Any Kind of Luck at All

any kind of luck at all

MARY FAIRHURST BREEN

Second Story Press

Library and Archives Canada Cataloguing in Publication

Title: Any kind of luck at all : a memoir / Mary Fairhurst Breen.
Names: Breen, Mary Fairhurst, 1963- author.
Identifiers: Canadiana (print) 20210143959 | Canadiana (ebook)
   20210144149 | ISBN 9781772602012 (softcover) | ISBN
   9781772602029 (EPUB)
Subjects: LCSH: Breen, Mary Fairhurst, 1963- | LCSH: Mothers—
   Biography. | LCSH: Mothers and daughters—Biography. | LCSH:
   Adjustment (Psychology) | LCSH: Resilience (Personality trait) |
   LCGFT: Autobiographies.
Classification: LCC HQ759 .B74 2021 | DDC 306.874/3—dc23

Cover by Natalie Olsen

Cover photo: Goce Ilievski / Stocksy.com

Versions of "Take Back the Night" and "Ms. Manners" have previously
appeared in *TROU Lit Magazine*. A version of "Graywood Drive" was
published in the anthology *What's Your Story?* through a partnership
among the Ontario Book Publishers Organization, Arts Etobicoke, and
the Toronto Arts Council. Portions of "Number Twelve" are adapted
from the CBC *The Sunday Edition* radio essay "Grievous Injuries."

Printed and bound in Canada

*Second Story Press gratefully acknowledges the support of the Ontario Arts
Council and the Canada Council for the Arts for our publishing program.
We acknowledge the financial support of the Government of Canada
through the Canada Book Fund.*

 ONTARIO ARTS COUNCIL
CONSEIL DES ARTS DE L'ONTARIO

 Canada Council   Conseil des Arts
for the Arts   du Canada

Funded by the Government of Canada
Financé par le gouvernement du Canada

 Canada

Published by
Second Story Press
20 Maud Street, Suite 401
Toronto, Ontario, Canada
M5V 2M5
www.secondstorypress.ca

MIX
Paper from
responsible sources
FSC® C103567

For Emma

contents

Foreword:
Any Kind of Luck at All

For years, one of my daughters or I would joke, "Uh oh, this is going in the book!" Sometimes it was more like, "Well, fuck, *this* is definitely going in the book." There was no book at the time, but as our adventures and misadventures accumulated, it began to feel like there might need to be one.

The first, very raw, draft of what would eventually become this memoir spewed out of me over the course of five days at the end of 2014, during which I never took off my pyjamas. It coincided with a rare but severe depression relapse. Needing to write during that wintry week felt a lot like needing to barf, but not wanting the unpleasantness. Once it was over, it was a huge relief.

What I thought I had made was a document for my daughters that might answer some of the spoken and unspoken questions swirling around us at the time. I hoped it would explain how things had gone so terribly wrong. My original audience was just these two people. I also embarked on a project to digitize and caption images from my huge collection of family photos and ephemera. All I felt I had going for me at the time was the strength of my foremothers. I couldn't fix anything, but I could at least try to share that with my children.

My therapist once told me, "You know, I don't think I've ever met anyone with worse luck than you." His point being that I shouldn't blame myself for all the things that have gone awry; only some are the direct result of my life choices. My dad liked the old chestnut, "If it weren't for bad luck, I wouldn't have any luck at all!" Maybe it's the Irish thing; after all, on the Breen side, my story begins with a famine.

I'd like to emphasize that plenty of people have far worse luck than me. I have always had loads of white and middle-class privilege, good food, access to health care, and a roof over my head, though the dwelling underneath it has become less commodious over time.

I have, however, experienced a series of rather momentous clusterfucks and a few cruel losses. I have bollocksed my selection of spouses. I have spent quite a while hovering around the poverty line. I have had to parent mostly unassisted. I have been a mother significantly longer than I had a mother, which has landed me in uncharted territory, where the landscape and its inhabitants can seem rather hostile.

What I inherited from my mother, my grandmother, and all the generations of aunts I never met is the ability to cope. I have coped, inelegantly but adequately, with everything that has walloped me so far. My foremothers' creativity, humour, resilience, and gentleness have given me what power I have to either fight or accept each new shitty development (and perhaps to fully enjoy the good ones too). At this moment in history, when the refusal of reality is wreaking havoc globally, I am especially grateful for this gift.

Annie, Andy, and Andie

FOR A GUY WHO tried to die repeatedly throughout the 1970s, my dad had a good innings. He made it past eighty, outliving my mum by almost seventeen years. She'd have been amazed.

I still unconsciously sprinkle my sentences with made-up words and arcane British expressions, like "had a good innings." I must have picked them up from my maternal grandmother. She lived with us briefly, and I remember her reading aloud lots of "bukes" (that's "books" with a Lancashire accent), as I snuggled into her absent bosom, flattened by a double mastectomy.

I'm "chuffed" when things go well, and "gobsmacked" by surprises. When visiting a new neighbourhood, I like to have a "gruzzle." If you almost run me down while I'm cycling, you may get a stern "Flippin' heck!" I still use my grandma's century-old secretary desk; it's moved with me a good dozen times. It's small, with only a hinged surface to work on, but I did all my translation assignments on it in university, huge dictionaries propped on top and on the floor around me. My fondness for grammar and language has never abated. I don't conjugate verbs as a form of meditation like she did, but I do play Scrabble to relax whenever I get the chance.

I remember my grandmother as rather sombre, influenced no doubt by her customary stern photo pose. One story that struck me was that she would do the dishes right after dinner without fail; she would not make an exception on holiday with the family in Ogunquit, Maine, even though it meant missing out on the sunset the others had gathered to enjoy on the beach. I spent a long time missing sunsets myself.

I do remember playing for hours with her magical button bag. The buttons would become characters—a grey elephant in the jungle, a fancy lady serving tea—or we would sort them in every imaginable way: size, colour, texture, temperament. I still have that purple Seagram's drawstring sack, now faded to a greyish-mauve, and I keep adding buttons to it. When I pick it up, I am five years old again, entranced by a handful of little discs.

My older cousins remember the infamous "Bad Manners Night," which happened from time to time when they were little, and throughout my mother's childhood as well. My grandmother was an absolute stickler for etiquette, with a knowledge of cutlery protocols to rival a Victorian footman. Table manners would have been symbolic of my grandparents' upward mobility—an indication they had made something of themselves. According to family lore, my grandmother brooked no slouching, talking out of turn, inelegant chewing, or fork offences. However, on bad manners night, she not only slurped her soup, but wiped her mouth on her sleeve! Elbows were brazenly planted on the table, and on one occasion, right in the gravy. My grandfather was known to flick peas at his young dinner companions.

Like many immigrants, he came to Canada several years ahead of his fiancée to establish himself. My grandmother joined him in 1916, stepping off the boat in Quebec City and marrying him that very day, as one could not spend the night with a man other than one's husband. She never got used to Canada; you can feel her homesickness in the postcards she sent to relatives back in England, wintry Krieghoff-style scenes on the front.

My grandmother's life transformed when she won a full scholarship to study at Bury Grammar School, an excellent private institution that paved her entrance into Manchester University (then Victoria University of Manchester) not long after it first admitted women. She completed a degree and teaching certificate, and became assistant headmistress at a girls' school, instead of working in the cotton mills like her sisters. Her family would have been described as "respectable working class." Her father was a stoker for the railroad; he lost an arm in a workplace accident but continued to be employed in other capacities. They lived in a "two up, two down" row house. Her four siblings were proud of "their" Rhoda and the older ones contributed to her tuition from their earnings.

My grandmother was an accomplished mathematician, about a hundred years before the kerfuffle over Teen Talk Barbie's lament, "Math class is tough!" Her major was Latin (hence her command of verbs). She named her springer spaniel Gloria in Excelsis Deo (Glo for short). Both she and my mother were pioneering when it came to their education. It was my intention to match or exceed their academic achievements.

At my mother's memorial, her classmate Sharon talked about how my mum had set the standard in the bacteriology department at McGill. What they must have endured as the only two women in their graduate science program, more than seven decades ago. I love the few snapshots I have of my mum on campus, and in her lab. Cat's eye glasses and pearls accessorizing her white coat, a cigarette burning in an ashtray set among the petri dishes or dangling from her lips as she peers into a microscope. My mother's graduate thesis, on the anaerobic flora of the upper respiratory tract, was prefaced by a quote from an Odgen Nash poem: "Do you, my poppet, feel infirm? You probably contain a germ."

My mother's flair for whimsy upset my tidy little mind as she strayed outside the lines of my colouring books, adding gratuitous doodles and embellishments. I wanted the pages to be *perfect*. I'd give anything to see one of those pictures now. Twenty years on, when her brain tumour had reached a certain size, she started colouring right onto the bed sheets with her little granddaughter by her side. One day she drew Hulk Hogan—who knows where he came from—and laughed and laughed as she captivated my toddler with a nonsensical story to go with her illustration.

The trousseaux my grandmother brought to Canada showcased the artistic talent passed down through generations of women in my family. It would seem my great- and great-great-aunts never let a bolt of cloth pass through their hands without adorning it with delicate needlework. I ended up with so many embroidered tablecloths I cut up a few to make bunting and other art pieces. I even smashed some of my great-aunt Annie's enormous set of intricately hand-painted china to make mosaics for my daughters a hundred years later.

I wish I had memories of my maternal grandfather —though his penchant for haggling is in my DNA. He reportedly tried to bargain everywhere, even at major department stores. I recall an excursion to Eaton's with my daughters to buy bridesmaid footwear; I aggrieved both my children and the poor hapless shoe department employee with my cheerful but persistent suggestion that I receive a volume discount on two pairs of Mary Janes and some black pumps. Flustered, the salesclerk kept disappearing to confer with his supervisor, with promises to return in "two shakes of a lamb's tail." Unable to pretend they weren't with me while trying on shoes, my daughters kept whisper-screaming "Muuuum!" and rolling their eyes. But we got fifteen per cent off and were ever after prone to fits of giggles at the expression "two shakes of a lamb's tail."

It wasn't chance so much as my grandfather's direct intervention that shaped my mother's life. When she was still a teen, he dismissed her goal of becoming a fashion designer as "frivolous." The way she explained it, he didn't mean to crush her dream; he just thought she was made for more intellectual pursuits. That may be true, but some of those outfits she made herself in the forties and fifties sure were spectacular.

When my mum was twenty-one, her father decided to tell her—after much soul-searching, she insisted—that her fiancé, Ray, was lazy. He worked at the paper mill where my grandfather had risen from the shop floor to upper management. Ray was dashing and charismatic, and such a fine dancer...but to an immigrant whose work ethic was his proudest asset, idleness must have been a deal-breaker. My mother called off the wedding, threw herself into work, and barely dated for the remainder of her twenties and thirties. Fast forward forty years and I heard my dad call my betrothed "a fart in a windstorm," but my mum voiced no objection when I married a guy a lot like Ray.

Replacing Ray proved no easy feat but replacing fashion design happened serendipitously. Filling a hole in her academic schedule with biology, my mother discovered a passion for microscopic life forms that probably made her as happy in a lab coat as she might ever have been in haute couture.

My mum went off to the metropolis of Montreal to attend McGill University at the age of sixteen. The war was on and there weren't enough teachers left to offer Grades 12 and 13 at her English high school in Trois Rivières. Men mostly taught the upper grades, while elementary school was the exclusive domain of women. She and her cohort were simply graduated after Grade 11. In her university dorm, the girls were closely supervised. The residence matron laid down the law: "Ten o'clock curfew, no male callers except Saturday evening, at least one foot in contact with the floor at all times."

I know little about my mum's dating life during the years between Ray and my dad, though I did hear about an incident in which she was chased around a couch by a suitor, unsuccessfully, because his legs were shorter than hers. It was told as a funny anecdote, but it sounds to me like a memorable-but-decidedly-unfunny attempted rape.

There is evidence of some socializing in the form of a marvelous letter sent to my mum and her sister, who were sharing accommodation in a boarding house in 1945. It would seem they had committed the offence of entertaining male guests in their room:

Having ascertained that you don't care much for the atmosphere of quietness and dignity of this house, and having no intention of lowering our standard, it seems that it will be better for all concerned that you will give your notice to take effect at the end of this month. We are certain that you easily can find a place less old fashioned and more to your liking.

It's very modern the way my mum looked up from her test tubes one day and noticed that her fallopian tubes were raising quite a ruckus. Along came Lloyd—book-smart, employed, and a suitable source of baby batter. I get it. She was pushing forty, so even though his only form of social intercourse was to tell jokes, she married him and got knocked up, almost in that order but not quite, by a margin of about three weeks. There I am, a secret little blastocyst under her beautifully tailored ivory silk suit at the wedding. I also get why she didn't wear her engagement ring at work. She said she just didn't want any fuss, and maybe in 1962 it was slightly embarrassing to be getting married for the first time at her age. But I'll bet she didn't want that diamond to serve as her notice of termination to her employer.

Professional women still hide their pregnancies until the last possible moment, as did she, aided by her considerable height and requisite lab coat. These days, though, her choice of a grilled cheese sandwich and a butter tart from the hospital cafeteria every day for lunch, a nightly glass of vermouth and a pack a day of Number Seven cigarettes would not be considered optimal prenatal care. These days, my father wouldn't leave her with a box of chocolates from the hospital gift shop and go home to await news of my arrival. These days, she would almost certainly have heeded all his bright red flags, and maybe even chosen to have a kid on her own.

I like it when I see her name—Andy—handwritten on the inside cover of books that migrated to my shelves. It also rankles me, because she agreed to switch to Anne at my father's request when they got married. Nobody called her Anne, not even her terribly proper parents. He also made the unilateral decision to move us to the suburbs over my mum's objection that Toronto—and civilization as we know it—ended at Jane Street. How foreign our tidy housing development must have felt, with its bucolically named streets leading nowhere, after the downtown flat she shared with a succession of friends who decamped one by one to become wives.

The name thing grated on me more as I got older, and I also became concerned, at the age of eleven, that my grandmother's maiden name was not going to live on, at least not on this side of the Atlantic. I don't know why this seemed so wrong to me as a kid, but I decided I needed to keep the matriline going. One couldn't just fill out some online forms to acquire a new moniker; I had to appear in court. It was terribly exciting. The judge asked me why I wanted to add Fairhurst to my name. I gave him my unconsciously mini-feminist, well-rehearsed answer, "Because my grandma's name will disappear if I don't take it."

Many years later, my mind was blown a little when I learned that our family tree has been traced back as far as one Margaret Fairhurst, who gave birth to a son out of wedlock in 1827, thus giving him her own last name. Her son Edward's birth certificate says, "father unknown," but a genealogist cousin has identified him as Henry, the village cobbler. Five generations later, it ended up on my ID, which I somehow feel retroactively legitimizes that illegitimate boy. Sweeter still, I now have a granddaughter named Andie.

Graywood Drive

ON GRAYWOOD DRIVE in the sixties and seventies, the mothers didn't work, and our most exotic neighbour had a vaguely Eastern European accent. The kids ran loose from the time we'd finished our Cap'n Crunch in the morning until the streetlights came on at night. Like the other mothers, mine made Hamburger Helper, ironed in front of *General Hospital,* and probably washed down a Valium with some gin every endless afternoon. Unlike them, she didn't care for bridge, so missed out on a key weekly social engagement.

There was a pleasantly non-hierarchical system among the kids. We all played Red Rover and British Bulldog up and down the unfenced yards and jumped through somebody's sprinkler when we got hot. One or another of the mothers would feed us hot dogs or egg salad sandwiches (white bread, no crusts) at lunchtime.

We raced homemade go-karts down the middle of the street and routinely climbed up on the school roof at the end of the block to retrieve our Frisbees.

The neighbourhood kids played together every day after school, but we didn't acknowledge each other within the walls of that institution, where strict social boundaries were in force. My fate was sealed in Grade 2, when my teacher made me mark my classmates' worksheets and spelling quizzes at her desk, while she read stories aloud and the kids took turns massaging her bunions. A few awkward girls were my friends. These were the girls picked last for the teams in gym class, as likely to take a ball in the glasses as catch it, like me. We all had good imaginations and spent a lot of time making up sketches and skits to entertain ourselves. I bet they all went on to do interesting, useful things.

I was saddled with my "browner" status right through elementary school. What popularity I had hinged on the good graces of Judy Atkin. She lived in a planned neighbourhood called Thorncrest Village—a kind of social experiment in snootiness, like an American gated community, but with fewer guns and more key parties. We lived just outside its boundaries. Good thing too. I can't see my dad flopping around on a waterbed with somebody else's wife.

One glorious day at the end of Grade 7, I was invited to a party with the cool kids, thanks to Judy's intervention on my behalf. I remember it was on the street where Toronto's disgraced former mayor, Rob Ford, later lived.

I contributed my portable turntable, which played both forty-fives and thirty-threes. My mother had won it in a contest, and it was the best gadget in our house. This party had everything: Pillsbury crescent roll hot dogs, Pop Shoppe soft drinks, slow dancing, and Seven Minutes in Heaven in the storage room with whichever gangly boy the spinning bottle indicated.

Necking was a hugely popular pastime for twelve- and thirteen-year-olds (this was before the advent of video games). These soirées continued every weekend, in similarly panelled rec rooms with green or orange shag carpeting. And I continued to be invited. At one of these parties, a boy named Peter had a go at squeezing my little apricot boobs during a Gino Vannelli song. I moved his hand around to the small of my back. He made a second attempt to cop a feel, which I also thwarted. After the song was over, I needed to spill the beans and I made the mistake of telling a member of the "in" crowd named Barbara. Barbara told one of the boys, who told the others, who rallied around their bro, accusing me of making it all up. And thus ended my season in the sun, as suddenly as it had begun. Call it my #MeTooJunior moment.

My fall from grace was quite breathtaking. It was decreed by the leader of the pack, a prematurely busty girl named Carol, that no girls were to speak to me. But my best friend Leanne did anyway. She hadn't been at the party, or I would have told her about the groping, and she would have believed me. We played the cello next to each other in strings and hung out while one or the other of us was babysitting on weekends, sampling all the kinds of booze in the families' wet bars.

There was a steep hill next to the school playground that got very icy in winter, and it was the habit of the cliques with power to send kids they wished to humiliate hurtling down the slope before the bell rang. I would start the school day damp, freezing, and bruised, but adults didn't get involved in these types of shenanigans back then, and no kid would think of snitching to a teacher.

I was mostly able to shake my untouchable status when I went to a big high school. I was determined not to be pigeonholed as a nerdy girl, so I refused my math teacher's offer to join the school's *Reach for the Top* team, which would compete on a televised academic quiz show. Canada's future prime minister, Stephen Harper, was the team captain. My teacher really wanted a girl on the team, and I should have been honoured to be asked when I was only in Grade 9, but I saw it as the kiss of death.

I found high school insufferably boring, so I stopped going very often. I found I could ace my exams with independent study and preferred to spend my days at the museum or the art gallery. Since my marks remained high, my mum didn't object. It wasn't that I was exceptionally smart; I just had a knack for memorization like my dad. Everything I learned fled my brain as soon as I'd regurgitated it onto a test sheet. I was more interested in literature and languages anyway, prompting my empirically inclined mother to tease, "You don't actually know any *facts*, do you?" But she wrote me notes to get out of detention, making up creative excuses for my absences.

I eventually switched to an alternative high school where the history classroom had floor cushions instead of chairs, the walls were covered with graffiti, and everyone was welcome to smoke in class. When John Lennon was shot, the students and teachers wore black armbands. We had women's studies three full decades before it was added to Ontario's high school curriculum. A classmate who later became a TV star told *People* magazine he had attended a school for social pariahs, which wasn't inaccurate. I loved it there. I devoured Hermann Hesse, Maya Angelou, Margaret Atwood, Alice Munro, and Jack Kerouac.

When I was seventeen, something snapped, and instead of being angsty in the manner of my literary heroes, I started getting panic attacks that scared the bejesus out of me. They must have terrified my mother too, but she spoke soothingly to me until they passed. Sometimes these incidents would involve wailing, and my father would stomp down the stairs to my room to ask, "What the hell is going on here?" He seemed annoyed that I was disturbing his daily twenty-two-hour nap, but I'm sure he was worried. Sometimes I had that bottom-of-a-pit feeling that causes people to take whole bottles of pills. One evening, that's what I did.

I immediately felt sheepish and skulked into the kitchen to tell my mother. I don't remember what I took, but whatever pre-Prozac antidepressant I was on would have been the only thing at hand. My mum was always good in a crisis. She calmly prepared a revolting mustard mixture to make me throw up. She put me in the car to go to the hospital. Unfortunately, she woke my father and brought him along. He kept muttering that I should be admitted, but I was released as soon as I'd ejected an adequate number of pills into a kidney bowl, which didn't take long, thanks to my mum's wherewithal. It was by no means a suicide attempt; it was a gesture of rage and confusion. I had only a cursory understanding of the situation in our house. We were mostly pretending it was fine, but it really wasn't fine. For years, I had been performing well but seething all the time, growling in my head.

I wound up in hospital twice that spring, for about a week each time, when I just couldn't move a muscle, and my mother got too nervous. I was put on various sedatives and antidepressants that achieved three results: excessive napping, wicked constipation, and a constant metallic taste in my mouth. I was on an adult ward full of people experiencing psychotic episodes. I was mostly bemused. Sometimes I would be invited to talk to a nurse, who would sit smoking opposite me in a little alcove. Sometimes we were all trotted into a meeting room to collate and staple documents under the guise of occupational therapy.

I remember little else from this time except for the one terrible thing I did to my mother: I phoned home and told her I was sorry, but I wasn't able to keep living. In that moment, I did want to die. My plan was to step in front of a bus on Bay Street. Being a teenager, I was not terribly aware of or empathetic to others, such as the driver and passengers of that bus. My only regret was having to leave my mother, and I didn't want to do it without saying good-bye. Of course, she phoned the nursing station immediately and the staff scolded me, took away my clothes, and put me in a hospital gown to make it apparent I was a flight risk and not allowed off the locked ward.

Looking back through my mother's diaries, it would seem I did quite a few terrible things, lashing out at her in the way we do only to the people who love us unconditionally, and despite the fact that they are the people we are least angry with in the world. I wish I could have asked her how she managed, because inevitably it would be my turn.

When my blues first started, my family doctor told me to "pull up my socks." I can't imagine why my mother stuck with him. This was the same guy who later completely missed her lung cancer. My expensive psychiatrist just sat opposite me and remained absolutely silent during our sessions. It must have been the "in" thing for shrinks to do at the time. Despite ineffective treatment, I bounced back. Maybe I was checking to see if I was as sick as my dad. I wasn't.

I got a much better therapist, who taught me behaviour modification and let me know that not every teenager had an obsessive-compulsive, manic-depressive dad upstairs, and it was okay to be upset about that. He was a very small man who often sat sideways in his chair like a little kid, his legs dangling over the armrest in well-tailored pants. He talked to me like I was smart. I stopped taking drugs that didn't work, and didn't need medication again for a decade, by which time research had radically improved their variety and effectiveness. Now I take antidepressants like a diabetic takes insulin. It is no different than any other manageable illness.

Shortly after my second hospital stay, a letter arrived notifying me that I'd been accepted into a summer immersion program in the Black Forest region of Germany. I don't know if my mother was petrified or saw the potential in a foreign adventure, but she agreed I could go, and her faith in me gave me a powerful boost. I don't remember my father being consulted. I rarely saw him because he didn't come downstairs or go out much after his mother died. She was the only person he'd get out of bed for.

I took the trip, made friends, and started working on a plan to get away from Etobicoke as fast as I could. To that end, I zipped through my final two years of high school in one, working double-time to get all the necessary credits with an average that would assure me entrance into any university. Shortly after my eighteenth birthday, I left for France to work as an au pair and backpack around for a year. I became fluent in French, learned to like beer, admired art, met adventurous youth from around the world, ate food from street vendors in the wee hours, fell for an American from Idaho who wouldn't fuck me for religious reasons, intrepidly took overnight trains to save on accommodation, and wrote copiously in my journal. I began to thrive.

My mum and I missed each other terribly while I was gone. Our letters took three weeks to arrive, and long-distance calls cost a fortune, so we spoke only occasionally. She concocted a scheme to get herself the hell out of that house and Etobicoke too, albeit briefly, coming with her sister to meet me for a tour of Greece. My father alternately threatened to kill himself while my mother was away, and insisted he'd be fine. After much waffling, she got on a plane to Athens.

The trip was perfect. We rode donkeys on Santorini, met pelicans on Mykonos, drank ouzo and ate grape leaves my aunt proudly ordered in Greek, having carefully studied her phrasebook. The three of us succumbed repeatedly to fits of laughter, as often happened when we were together.

For years after my mother's death, whenever I would return to Toronto from a work-related trip or holiday, I would secretly hope there was a message waiting for me to let me know my father had died while I was away. To end his own suffering and mine. I wonder if my mother felt the same way as she got on her return flight from Greece.

Clams

IT PUZZLED MY MOTHER that my father still lived at home with his mother when they met. Nowadays, impecunious or divorced adult children return to the nest quite regularly, but back then it was highly irregular. Funnily enough, poking around on Ancestry.ca, I found out that my original Irish ancestor on my dad's side, who came to Canada in the mass migration, fathered seven kids with a woman named Fanny but wasn't living with her at the time of his death in 1901. He was living with his mother.

I've yet to uncover any evidence that my father dated before he was fixed up with my mum, though a much older cousin recalls a lovely woman who regularly came along when my dad took his nieces and nephews skating; the family expected them to marry. Perhaps he experienced heartbreak, just like my mum did. My cousins remember him as a jocular, playful uncle. Apparently, they would take great delight in tiptoeing into his room at my grandmother's house while he was sleeping, then start grinding pencils with the very loud sharpener attached to the bottom of his bed frame. He would pretend to be all outraged and befuddled. He spent a lot of time at his sister's cottage on Lake Simcoe, various nieces and nephews jumping off his shoulders into the water.

He never took me skating or paddled in a lake with me. I rarely saw him have fun. By the time I was born, he didn't do anything for pleasure, not that I remember. I can see him on our occasional family holidays, sitting stiffly in a lawn chair, still wearing his leather dress shoes on the beach or by the pool.

Now I know it was his burgeoning obsessive-compulsive disorder that made any change in routine so painful for him. He tried to rally when my mother organized a final holiday at Rice Lake the summer before she died. Normally he would have stayed home, but he did his best to endure a cottage with my mum, husband, daughter, and me. It was booked for two weeks. After a couple of days, he broke his leg stepping up a small sandy slope. That's how badly he needed to leave.

My mum did have one story about a grand romantic gesture, and it was a good one—my dad arranged a flight in a tiny propeller plane from Toronto to Niagara Falls for dinner in one of the fancy revolving restaurants. But when the day came to move into their first matrimonial home, his belongings were packed into a couple dozen plastic grocery bags from A&P. On their honeymoon in Prince

Edward Island, he nearly died from an allergic reaction to clams. The curious part is that he later acknowledged that this always happened when he ate clams.

"The last time I had sex with your father was January 1974," my mother told me, during the intermission of a Broadway show starring Sandy Duncan and Tommy Tune. She went on to confirm my suspicion that my dad was her one and only sexual partner (with Ray, she'd come "close as damn it"). We were having a mother-daughter weekend in New York, in January 1984. Her revelation made me think of the joke, "Such terrible food, and such small portions!" After Dad got testicular cancer, he declared his equipment broken (I've bonked a fellow who also lost a ball—his gear worked fine), and they slept in separate rooms.

I grew up thinking my father's side of the family lived in poverty, which is not untrue, but there is more to the story. They certainly struggled during the Depression, my grandmother taking in boarders, washing, and sewing, and reusing every scrap of fabric to clothe the kids. They sometimes had to scrounge or steal to eat, a job that fell to the two boys, who had an older and a younger sister at home, as well as a series of German shepherds, all called Duke. I think about that when I see street youth with intimidating dogs.

Dad's eldest sister, Velma, was sent to live with a rich aunt when she was an adolescent. I assumed there was a rich aunt through marriage, but it turns out she was a lifelong spinster. Velma had a chronic ear ailment, which was more than my grandmother could handle or afford with four smaller kids at home. I thought my grandmother grew up on the family farm in the Holland Marsh, and attended school only until Grade 8, but there are apparently photos of her playing tennis, which seems incongruous with my information. She said "warshing" instead of "washing," which seems incongruous with playing tennis. In any case, she and/or her husband clearly passed on some smarts.

My grandmother's father and brothers became very successful in the building business and later made good real estate investments, accumulating considerable wealth. A number of them were in lumber; going down a Google rabbit hole, I discovered that one of my dad's cousins sold his small lumber company to a huge national chain and started a charitable foundation still run by his heirs. All of this was very confusing until I finally uncovered the plot twist I'd been missing: my grandmother did not share in any of this prosperity because her family turned their backs on her when she married my grandfather. He had a gambling problem and lived only sporadically with his family. There are five kids, so the terrible family joke is that he popped by five times.

I never once heard my dad talk about his father. His mother eventually demanded that her sons kick him out of the house when they were still boys. I picture this taking place literally, like in a Western, my grandfather flying out the door and landing in some tumbleweed. I don't know what my grandfather looked like; I've never seen a picture. Mum said that Grandma B. didn't speak to her husband even when they were under the same roof; if she absolutely had to communicate, she wrote him a note. As a consequence, my dad would never write down so much as a phone message. He would just memorize the information to be relayed, including the caller's name and a phone number he'd heard only once. Dad had a severe stutter as a child. He cured it himself, by yelling limericks out into Lake Ontario.

My father was so determined to disassociate from his past that he never even told me about his uncle Joe Breen, a celebrated football player who was with the Argos immediately before and after World War I. He won a Grey Cup and was named to the Canadian Football Hall of Fame and the Canadian Sports Hall of Fame. Like my dad, he became an engineer and went into the cement business after his sports career ended. It's easy to find pictures of Joe online; he and my dad look astoundingly alike.

Velma grew up privileged but very lonely, isolated from her siblings. She enjoyed a good education and was very accomplished, as was her husband, a respected economist. Things started to unravel for her later in life, due to a combination of mental illness and alcoholism. The next sister, Joyce, was a flight attendant in the early days of air travel, which meant she also had to train as a nurse. She came down with depression, but not until very late in life, after a series of terrible personal losses. The youngest, Lois, was probably tied for most ill with my dad; she spent time at Lakeshore Psychiatric Hospital as a young woman. She married a World War II vet who had what they called "shell shock," from his time in a Japanese POW camp. She and her husband spent their days companionably watching game shows together and doting on their dog. They dyed the grey out of each other's hair to stay young-looking. Lois said to anyone who would listen that she had the best husband a girl could ask for, and you could tell she really meant it.

Dad and his brother Ross figured out early on that their exit route was an education. The only story my dad would repeatedly tell from his youth concerned his near-perfect high school grades. He remembered his exact mark in each of his Grade 13 subjects, ranging from ninety-seven to one hundred per cent. His eyes were firmly on the prize—a full scholarship to university. In the summers, he and Ross worked the harshest and most hazardous construction jobs, because those paid top dollar. The one thing Dad would say about this experience was that his pale Irish skin would turn the colour of a Hershey bar by the end of each season. He would take off his shirt for incrementally longer periods each day to avoid burning to a crisp. He liked to mimic the action of unwrapping the chocolate and putting it up against his chest to compare.

Once he'd made it, my father never picked up a tool again. For him, there was only indignity in manual labour. He sought comfort in modern conveniences. A getaway to a rustic cabin was his idea of wretchedness, not a vacation. Our driveway was never shoveled and our lawn never mowed until some enterprising boy came by to offer his services. My mother or I could have done it, but those weren't girls' jobs. It would have been even more embarrassing for us to get out there with the mower than to have shin-deep grass. I grew accustomed to asking Mr. Dixon at the end of the street to fix my bike when I got a flat or needed the handlebars raised. I remember waking him one day when Dad was in hospital, unaware he'd just finished a night shift as a beat cop. He liked to tell stories at block parties about roughing up vagrants at Cherry Beach, but he was nice to me. Everyone was, because Dad was in the loony bin. That much the neighbours knew.

I'm guessing my mother didn't tell me about half my father's suicide attempts, but I do remember the phone ringing, then my mother hastily depositing me with one or another of the neighbours while she dashed to the hospital. I'd hang out there, watching *Happy Days* and playing Crazy Eights with the kids until she returned.

Some years later, she told me that on one of these occasions, he escaped the psych ward and tried to drown himself in Lake Ontario, but his swimming training kicked in and he couldn't help saving himself. He'd learned to swim in the lake at Sunnyside Park, during its heyday as a recreation spot. He rode his bike or hitchhiked in from Mimico. He learned from Gus Ryder, who went on to fame as Marilyn Bell's coach when she made her historic lake crossing in the fifties. He was proud of his swimming ability, and it was the one thing he insisted I learn.

Packing up my parents' condo a few years after my mum died, I found my dad's old hunting rifle in the back of a closet. He'd tried hunting only a few times but couldn't stomach it. I discreetly turned the gun in to the local police. I wonder if he knew the bullets had been removed by an outdoorsy family friend years earlier. I remember Mr. Grant coming to the house once when my dad was in hospital, but I didn't know why until sometime later when my mum explained what he'd done.

After his long hospital stays came the years my dad spent all day in bed. At dinnertime, he would emerge to wolf down a meal in front of the TV news, then phone his mother. The love/hate dynamic between Dad and Grandma B. made for a cacophonous soundtrack to our dinner every night, as he bellowed at her about going to the mall on the weekend. The phone was attached to the kitchen wall, so the bellowing took place where my mum and I ate. My grandmother always argued that she didn't want to go shopping, but every Saturday morning, though he'd been incapacitated all week, Dad would shower, dress, pick her up from her nursing home, stick her in the wheelchair he had bought for the purpose, and push her around the mall with dogged determination. Mum and I weren't invited and never tagged along.

My father and grandmother would come back to our house for tea very occasionally. My grandmother would have me climb on a chair to put her purse on top of a high cabinet, so the kids couldn't reach in and get her pills. The thing is, I was the only kid anywhere in the vicinity. My mum would find something to do in the kitchen when they started pulling out the pretty nighties and dresses my dad had bought for his mother.

Clearing out my mum's room after her death, I unearthed a letter from Aunt Velma. My dad gave me this job, and wanted it done quickly. As I separated her clothes into piles to donate, he'd pop his head in and say, "That must be hard." I wonder if my mum knew the letter was still there. It was among her complete set of diaries dating back thirty years, neatly stacked on a shelf in her closet. Some were simply notes scrawled on free promotional calendars, others longer entries in school scribblers or dime store notebooks. There were a lot of quotidian records among the more personal stuff. Lists of the toys I'd received for Christmas (and would be required to acknowledge by letter no later than Boxing Day), shopping lists that included such items as Instant Breakfast, Minute Rice, and Jell-O. Entries from the early sixties noted what kind of day I was having (M no nap, cranky). Later entries noted what kind of a day my dad was having (L in bed all day, acting mean).

I read my aunt's letter sitting on the walk-in closet floor. It was dated shortly after my parents' wedding, too late to serve as a warning. Velma writes, as candidly as decorum would have permitted, about the "sick" relationship between Dad and Grandma B. Velma's behaviour could be quite erratic and harmful, particularly after she was widowed in her early fifties; she wrought considerable havoc when she was binge drinking. It's quite possible she fabricated or embellished her revelation. It's also possible that she didn't.

My mum had alluded to her suspicions a few times as I grew older, first too vaguely for me to catch on at all, then more pointedly. She said my dad and grandmother had shared a bedroom at some point. She told me it made her cringe when he blithely walked in on his mother changing, and even helped her dress. But I was still ill-prepared for this written eyewitness account. I did not mention it to my dad, of course, and the letter went into the bin. I did mention it to my cousins during one of our occasional brunches. Velma's daughter is twenty years older than me and had much more time with our grandmother, whose very mention sets her teeth on edge. She said, "It's a wonder any of us are still standing."

Uncle Ross had an aptitude for science and chose dentistry. Family members got a small discount at his practice, but he apparently wouldn't fix Lois's dentures for free, even though they clattered around in her mouth. My mum was disinclined to speak ill of anyone, but I remember that made her mad. True or not, it's a fact that everyone is weird about money, especially if you've never had it and then do, or always had it and then don't. My uncle and his wife also made rude remarks about my teen attire and funny coloured hair, which caused my mum to snark, "You can't tell me *her* hair colour doesn't come from a bottle." Depression got Ross too. After my mum and his wife were gone, he and my dad might have offered comfort to one another, but instead they argued like ten-year-old boys and took turns blocking each other's phone numbers until they ceased speaking at all. When Ross died, after a few years of fraternal silence, my dad went back to bed for a couple of weeks. He unintentionally outlived all his siblings.

Dad demonstrated that he was no longer broke with gestures of largesse. Before his illness, these were welcome acts of kindness. He gave Velma's daughter fifty bucks in one-dollar bills when she was struggling to pay her way through university. That was a lot of money in the late fifties; how thoughtful to present it in singles she could pull out for a meal here, a textbook there.

Later, my dad would lavish people he barely knew with gifts such as opera and baseball tickets. He always picked up the tab, even when it was socially awkward to do so. When he was still going out, he'd invite an assortment of acquaintances to an old-school steak-and-potatoes type of restaurant and spend an outlandish sum of money on food and drink. He tended to collect oddballs who enjoyed his largesse for limited periods of time. After my jewellery box was stolen during a break-in at my apartment in Montreal, he would send me a carefully wrapped Kleenex box every week for several months. In it would be much of the original Kleenex, surrounding a small box containing earrings. Always real gold or silver, always feminine and tasteful, always the opposite of my style. I remember one very uncomfortable Christmas, when my dad wouldn't come to my aunt's house in Kingston with us but bought me a beautiful opal ring with matching earrings (these I loved) and my mum an ostentatious sapphire ring that she hated.

His purchase of an investment property in the seventies coincided with his first major manic episode in what would turn out to be a chronic and largely untreatable case of bipolar disorder. He installed the most expensive fixtures that money could buy, right down to the light switches and doorknobs. Since it was my mother's money he was doling out, when he lost it all and came crashing down from his emotional high, his shame was overwhelming.

Mum told me that when medical professionals would ask Dad a question, he would either sit in stony silence, or tell them one of the dozen, ancient jokes in his repertoire. (*I passed a farm the other day and saw a goat with no nose. I said to the farmer, "How does he smell?" The farmer said, "Terrible!"*) He was mostly compliant about taking his medication, but the years of agonizing illness and multiple rounds of electroconvulsive therapy took a huge toll.

For periods, he would look and smell like someone with no access to hot running water. In his final decade, he wouldn't put on a coat or hat in the winter, but he didn't really go anywhere, so it wasn't that big a deal. He took a cab to the grocery store in Thorncrest Plaza by our old house on Graywood Drive to buy the bananas he ate every day. He wouldn't go into the fruit stores on his block, and it was no use bringing him bananas. They weren't the right ones, and he would let them rot until someone from maintenance had to come deal with the fruit flies.

When I was a baby, Dad claimed he had to travel constantly for work, but later confessed that he sought out those assignments in mining communities in the far north. I guess he didn't know what to make of my squalling interruption to his routine. It's hard to say if he was displaying early signs of the mental illnesses to come, or just behaving like the man of the house. Luckily for all of us, he moved over to the civil service before he got really sick. We had a safety net to break our fall, complete with indefinite disability benefits, an indexed pension, and life-long health coverage that included the round-the-clock palliative care my mother would eventually need.

I remember only a few occasions when I spent time alone with Dad as a kid. I have a very early, very happy memory of sitting on his lap and repeating the names of items in the Eaton's catalogue. He wanted me to learn to navigate the subway system, which is sensible, but he went a bit overboard by making me memorize all the subway stops as a very young child, during excursions that served no other purpose than these lessons. I sat in the very front of the train, watching as we sped through the tunnels. After each stop, he'd ask, "What's next?" and I'd rhyme off the names of the stations from west to east: "Royal York! Old Mill! Jane!" I remember being pleased when he praised me for getting them right. I can still recite all the stops on the Bloor and Yonge-University lines, excluding stations added since 1970.

Around the same period as the subway outings, we'd sometimes go for a Saturday morning walk through

Islington golf course to Country Style Donuts, where he would have a coffee and I would get a French cruller while my mum slept in. I remember really loving these adventures, which I thought started so early it was practically still the middle of the night. I walked a long way on my five- or six-year-old legs. Dawdling wouldn't have been an option.

Sometimes we ended up at the beauty parlour in Thorncrest Plaza. Dad would pay to have my hair teased and sprayed into a fashionable beehive and wait patiently while the transformation was performed. My fine, stringy hair would be drooping within hours, but I thought it was great fun. How is it there are no photos of these 'dos? In fact, my parents took only a handful of pictures of me during my whole childhood. Some years ago, I finally got to the bottom of a huge bin of ephemera, photos and slides, and found a small box labelled, "Poor Mary." It contained adorable baby pictures I'd never seen before. I look pudgy and smiley, though I am noticeably cross-eyed, due to a case of amblyopia that would need fixing. I have no idea who wrote "Poor Mary." It doesn't look like either of my parent's handwriting.

The only other time I recall being on my own with Dad was when I was eight, and Mum was hospitalized with a bleeding ulcer. My mother was suffering from agoraphobia, and no wonder: she was a stranger in a strange suburban land. She got down to a skeletal hundred and fifteen pounds on a five-foot-ten frame, consuming only milk and cigarettes, which the nurses took away from her and smoked, much to her consternation. While she was in hospital, Dad fed me at the diner in Thorncrest Plaza. I had a grilled cheese sandwich and chocolate milk for every meal. It was Christmas holidays, so to pass the time, he took me to movies at the Westwood Theatre. It didn't matter what was playing, or whether it had a G or R rating. We walked in at whatever time we arrived, even if the movie was half over, and then sat through the first part of the next screening to get our money's worth. It was how my dad always watched movies.

My mother never fully wrested control of their finances from my father, maybe because that too was men's work. A few years after she died, I discovered that he hadn't been paying his taxes, so I gingerly asked if I could take over, and he was visibly relieved. His world was very small, but he got by as long as he didn't have to face anything out of the ordinary and could stick to a precise routine. He got out of bed almost every day and visited the girls and me alternate Sundays for exactly ninety minutes.

Mum wouldn't leave Dad because she was afraid of two catastrophic results—her poverty, and his suicide. I think it's safe to say neither of those things would have happened. Not to her, anyway.

My mother went to her first job interview at the age of fifty-five. She was recruited right out of McGill by the Montreal Children's Hospital, then headhunted by the Toronto Hospital for Sick Children in the early fifties. But bacteria mutate fast; having been away from the workforce for more than fifteen years, she couldn't go back to the lab with such outdated scientific knowledge. She had taken up behaviour therapy, kind of as a hobby, after her own successful treatment for agoraphobia. (I can picture her Post-It notes, stuck inside cupboards all around the house, that read, "Calm, Confidence, Courage, Serenity.") She threw herself into volunteering at Lakeshore Psychiatric Hospital, leading peer support groups for people with anxiety.

My mum gained a new lease on life when she answered an ad for a medical secretary. She left for downtown each morning, in a sharp outfit and stylish shoes, a spring in her step. The job wasn't hard; she enjoyed colour-coding files and making columns of numbers add up. She ran that practice with sublime efficiency. I would meet her for cappuccinos when I was back from my gap year and living near the university.

I don't recall my mother being politically engaged when I was a kid. But the arms race got her seriously riled up, as the potential vaporization of all the world's inhabitants would do to a person. I was glad when she found kinship among the older peace activists at Voice of Women. Her actions had been as defiant and principled as any of these women's exploits, but she'd never really identified with the women's movement before making the connection between feminism and anti-militarism. We had some good times protesting together in her final years. She was chuffed when I got arrested for civil disobedience.

I was twenty-five when my mother had surgery for a herniated disc that was causing trouble in her hips and legs. While she was laid up in the hospital, I used her ticket to see Lily Tomlin in *The Search for Signs of Intelligent Life in the Universe*. I had a wonderful evening at the theatre sitting with her boisterous friends.

When I got home, my young husband was still up. He looked ashen. He told me my mum had phoned while I was out. "She has cancer," he said, and then there was a long interlude while we both cried. Slowly, he shared the details, as he'd been coached to do. What the doctors at the hospital initially thought was tuberculosis was, in fact, inoperable lung cancer. My mum's family doctor had seen shadows on her lungs a few years prior but dismissed them as scarring from a bout of pneumonia. We'd all known it wasn't tuberculosis; my mum always tested positive because of exposure at work in the lab. Visiting her in the hospital, we'd take our masks off as soon as the medical staff was out of sight. "The cancer has metastasized to her brain," my husband said.

My first, utterly selfish thought was that I was going to be stuck looking after my father. It turned out this was uppermost in her mind too. My mum set three short-term goals for herself, as part of an exercise in her cancer support group: to get arrested, to try marijuana, and to outlive her husband. She only reached one of them.

The distress of the next fifteen months was relentless. When my mum's sister died of ovarian cancer five months after her own diagnosis, it was like watching a trailer for the horror movie of our lives, soon to be released. My mum hadn't been able to tell her sister about her cancer; she'd had to ask her niece to do it, just as she'd asked my husband to tell me. It was too much to deliver news she knew would cause such profound sorrow to the people who loved and relied on her most.

There were ducks to put in a row. My mother and I planned her memorial from a hotel in Thunder Bay, where we were staying courtesy of the Ontario Health Insurance Plan while she received radiation treatment there. There was no officiant; my husband was the MC. Friends from each stage of her life shared memories, to create a winding narrative about a principled, brilliant, funny, loyal woman. One friend performed a beautiful song from Margaret Laurence's memoir, *Dance on the Earth*. Dad wasn't involved and didn't attend. He never could handle funerals.

In the run-up to Mum's inevitable death, Dad was paralyzed by fear. He relinquished all responsibility for her care to me. He threw money at the problem—the only strategy he'd ever employed in a crisis—pressing cash into my hand to pay for babysitters and house cleaners so I could care for her, just as he'd once paid for babysitters and house cleaners rather than help my mother care for me.

My mum had heard that weed could really help with chemo symptoms, so I got some quality product and baked it into our favourite sugar cookie recipe (she couldn't very well smoke it when she needed an oxygen tank just to take a full breath). The cookies were in a tin in the back seat the afternoon I drove her to a wig shop in the Hasidic Jewish part of the city. A tiny old lady, who should long since have given up driving, smashed into the back of my car while we were stopped at a light. As I waited for the cops, my mother made quite an impression, striding up to an Orthodox Jewish man filling up at a nearby gas station and asking if she could hitch a ride to the wigmaker's. Under no circumstances did my mother want to be late for her appointment. She climbed into his van full of kids and carried on. The tin of special treats went unnoticed as I filed my police report.

I warned her to take just a few bites of cookie and wait to see how she felt, but my mother reasoned that because she was so tall and could barely get tipsy on half a bottle of wine, she should eat two cookies. I was at work when my dad phoned to say, without a trace of levity, "Your mother is stoned." It's a shame she got herself so unpleasantly high, to the point of paranoia, and had to banish the rest of the batch to the freezer (my husband obligingly ate them later).

As my mother's brain tumour advanced, my dad didn't handle her confusion well; he berated her for it, which made me more livid than anything he'd ever done. One day she responded to this abuse by hurling overripe tomatoes at him, which was certainly something new. My father petulantly wore his tomato-stained shirt for several days. But not long after this food fight, she told me she had started crawling into bed with him most mornings, where they chatted and laughed. Voluntarily or involuntarily, her brain was dulcifying her bitterness.

I got a call at work one day from Grace Hospital, where a palliative care bed had become available; they needed an immediate answer as to whether we wanted it. I tried to have a phone conversation with my mum about it, but she was no longer clear where she was, and kept losing the receiver in the bedsheets. Dad insisted I decide what to do. My doctor had prescribed me some Ativan, and that was the day I started taking it.

Dad took the opportunity to die when he went into hospital for a routine hernia operation. That sounds medically implausible, but I'm sure it's true. When I left him at the Admitting Department that winter morning, he told me I'd been the best daughter he could have asked for. I tried to shrug it off. I told him I'd see him after work. I didn't feel like a good daughter, though I'd done what was required of me.

He seemed reasonably okay post-surgery, but the next day he didn't look right and said he was in pain. This was something, coming from a man who had an impossibly high pain threshold. (One time, he took the subway to work after slipping on the ice and breaking his ankle. He only agreed to go to Emerg when his secretary nearly fainted at the sight of it.) His surgeon couldn't figure out why Dad wasn't bouncing back and ordered some tests. When I came back after work, he was in the ICU, where a team of people had been trying for some time to kickstart his heart. I asked them to stop.

Charisma

THE HARDEST QUESTION my daughter Sophie ever asked me—and she came up with some doozies—was: "How could you have had children with Dad?" I tried to explain to my two daughters how their father's charm, his cooking, and his politics swept me off my feet. I was twenty, barely an adult, but terrified nobody else would ever love me. He loved me, loudly, messily, and thoroughly.

When I met him, Dan seemed everything my father was not. My dad had been either in hospital or in bed with crippling bipolar disorder and OCD from the time I was eleven. I didn't have any grandfathers or brothers, and my few uncles were distant and damaged in their own ways. My parents were not separated, but I was raised by a single mum. I had never known a fully functional, competent, independent man, or seen a healthy marriage up close.

We met getting arrested. It was the height of the Cold War, and we were protesting against the manufacturer of the cruise missile guidance system. The early eighties were a time of urgent activism for those of us frantic about the prospect of nuclear annihilation. There were lots of peace groups around, some more liberal, others more radical. I cut my teeth at the Toronto Disarmament Network and then moved on to the Alliance for Non-Violent Action.

Dozens of people were arrested during Remembrance Week 1983, climbing the fence at Litton Industries for the token purpose of making a citizen's arrest of the company's directors. Protesters self-organized into small "affinity groups;" ours formed because we happened to take the same non-violent resistance training together. We were a motley crew made up of a suburban teenager, a couple of punk young men, an old American pacifist, a West Coast hippie, my mum, and me. The night before the "action," we all got together to paint a dove my mother had designed onto vests fashioned from pillowcases. We called ourselves the "Planet Lovers," after Terre Nash's 1982 documentary, *If You Love This Planet*.

Ours was the third of three large protests that week. Each followed the same pattern: people climbed the company's fence into the waiting arms of police, went limp, and were dragged to a police van. (Going limp was standard protest protocol back then; apparently now it's considered resisting arrest, so, not recommended.) Dan made the front page of the *Toronto Star*, a cop hauling him by the elbows, his dove clearly displayed. Protesters were held briefly at 22 Division of Toronto Police Services in the middle of Etobicoke. Members of our affinity group went to my parents' nearby home for chili after being released. My mum wasn't ready to get arrested yet, so she was a "support person," taking care of the phone tree and such. She spoke to my future in-laws that day, telling them Dan had been charged with trespassing. His dad said, "Right on."

The following day, the younger participants in the week's protests had plans to celebrate our tiny triumph over the military-industrial complex. I was surprised when Dan offered to come meet me after my shift at the Eaton Centre to escort me to the party. I was more surprised when he showed up looking very dapper in a vintage suit and led me on a detour to a bar first, where he proceeded to tell me all about himself. It felt exactly like a first date, but I was terribly confused. I had assumed that Dan and his roommate Steve were a couple, because of their New Wave sartorial style (Dan had a single earring and hair the colour of Orange Crush). I'd been quite pleased to make some of my first gay friends.

Not only was Dan straight, handsome, and a feminist peace activist, but he badly wanted to get into my parachute pants. He said he'd had the hots for me straight away, but an article in the *Globe and Mail* had dismissed us anti-nuke protesters as a bunch of flakes looking to get laid, and he wanted to be taken seriously. That very night, he declared his love for me at Ossington subway station, where he had accompanied me hoping for an invitation back to my place. I couldn't process what was happening in the moment but was ready to consummate our relationship a couple of days later.

I'd had one serious boyfriend up to that point and a total of two sexual partners. Dan was directionless but a heck of a lot of fun. The sex was so emotional, it often brought one or both of us to tears. I suspect the passion changed my brain chemistry. Plus, he was a socialist. What more could a girl want? We started playing house immediately. While I was in class, Dan would hang around my apartment reading my books and smoking cigarettes he'd bought with the quarters in my laundry jar. He'd dropped out of university and was doing a bit of house painting but not much else. He'd stay out until dawn partying while I worried about the temptation of other girls, and at the same time admonished myself for losing sleep over a boy. When his antics had me at my wits' end, he had a knack for producing a candlelit dinner of perfectly roasted chicken, and sometimes even a poem.

I had doubts. I even had an affair some months after we'd started cohabiting, with the American from Boise, Idaho I'd met during my gap year in France. He hadn't believed in sex before marriage at the time, which was frustrating when we were backpacking through some of the most romantic settings in Italy, sharing a room in charming *pensioni* (family-run guesthouses). He'd changed his position after leaving home and settling in New Orleans, so I had copious amounts of sex with him in the bayou heat and considered my options. Here was evidence that it was possible for other smart, attractive men to want me, but I returned to Dan. I told him about my indiscretion as soon as I got back, and he didn't mind at all. He wasn't the jealous type, perhaps because he'd never been turned down by a woman and felt confident that he could have whomever he desired. I was grateful he chose me.

Dan followed me to Montreal where I wanted to continue my postsecondary education in a francophone environment because I was majoring in French translation. He decided to pick up his studies at the same university. We immediately became enmeshed in various peace groups and got ourselves arrested at the Department of National Defence within weeks of our arrival, still panicked about the nuclear arms race and Canada's role in it. Several of us in our new local Alliance for Non-Violent Action group had break-ins around the same time. The thieves took mostly papers, plus our few valuables, like my jewellery box. It was very inconvenient, as they nabbed a bunch of course notes and draft essays from our backpacks and desks, along with my well-organized personal files. Our theory was that CSIS (Canadian Security Intelligence Service) was behind it, hiring locals who could keep whatever spoils the government didn't want.

That sounds like ridiculous paranoia, but years later I wrote to CSIS to ask for my file, just out of curiosity. It had become well-known that they'd wasted time tracking all manner of feminists and pacifists for decades. My request cost me five dollars and a self-addressed envelope. I got a comically Big Brotherish letter back:

We neither confirm nor deny that the records you requested exist. We are, however, advising you… that such records, if they existed, could reasonably be expected to be exempted (from freedom on information laws)…as it relates to the efforts of Canada toward detecting, preventing or suppressing subversive or hostile activities.

Dan became smitten with another member of the Quebec Public Interest Research Group, whose meetings we attended weekly to tackle a host of social justice issues. He lied a lot about spending time at her apartment, though he said they weren't having sex. I wondered again about leaving him. But then he proposed, after a fashion.

I was in the bathtub, with the door open so we could chat while he was looking at the university course catalogue in the kitchen. He called out, "Says here if we get married by Labour Day, we can get grant money." Quebec has always had lower tuition and higher student subsidies than other provinces and, at the time, offered generous grants to any students who were independent of their parents. Independence was defined as having lived away from home for five years or being married. Many students cottoned on and married each other to take advantage of this loophole—roommates, friends, lesbians and gays, the two of us.

We didn't do it entirely under the radar since we were a real couple. We went to City Hall, then my parents threw us a small party at their condo. The catering bill was five hundred and fifty dollars—I found it later in the wedding album my mum put together. My dress was a hundred and sixty dollars, more than I had ever imagined an article of clothing could cost. We were kind of irreverent with our attire—I wore a vintage hat with a veil, and Dan wore a red bow tie—but I still wanted to look nice on my wedding day.

On the day before the ceremony, as I was ironing Dan's jacket and pants, my American lover called. A year had passed since our tryst, during which we'd exchanged letters. He'd visited at New Year's, but had stayed in our spare room, despite Dan's willingness to have a threesome. On the phone, he didn't say, "Don't do this." He said, "Are you really doing this?" I said I was. I can't say for sure whether a different question would have produced a different answer.

Two months later, on Dan's twenty-fifth birthday, we had this conversation:

"We're out of condoms!"

"Should we go ahead anyway? I'm ovulating!"

"Let's make a baby!"

Half an hour later, we'd done just that, fertile youngsters that we were. Within weeks, the vomiting was relentless; I missed my Christmas exams and had to write them in January when I was through my first trimester. I graduated in May and Emma was born in July, back in Toronto. Dan hadn't finished his degree. He'd gathered enough total credits, but switched majors so many times he didn't have the requisite courses in any one subject to graduate. He was, however, a knowledgeable and inter-esting conversationalist for his efforts. He completed a carpentry course during Emma's first year, while we lived on my contract work, the last of my education savings, and subsidies from my parents.

When Emma was just a few months old, I caught Dan in another web of lies and he revealed that he was in love with his friend's girlfriend: the daughter, it so happened, of a celebrated Canadian author, whose work I haven't been able to fully enjoy since. I had splurged on basketball tickets for his birthday, and at the game, he told me that when he and his inamorata saw each other, they "just knew." Again, he said the relationship hadn't been consummated, but the emotional betrayal was far worse. When I replay this scene in my head, I storm out of the stadium. In reality, I sat through the game and developed irritable bowel syndrome.

Having a baby was not a sensible thing to do, obvi-ously. Not with Dan, and not at twenty-three. I got plenty of sidelong glances from the mothers ten or fifteen years my senior at my prenatal yoga classes and postnatal drop-ins. But I was unequivocally glad I did it, especially when my mother was diagnosed with terminal cancer eighteen months later. Although she was given six months to live, she made it until Emma was almost four. She would say to me, "You're besotted with that child!" We all were—my mum and dad, Dan, and me.

When my mum was dying, before she lost her mind, I told her I thought I'd have to leave Dan, and her immediate response was, "I don't want you to be lonely." Maybe her fear of being alone had been the deciding factor in her reluctance to leave my dad, more powerful even than her fear of poverty or of his demise.

Struggling as we were to make ends meet and manage our lives, Dan and I thought we'd stop at one child. But after my mum's death, I had a gaping void to cope with and, more pragmatically, a desire to give Emma a sibling. I'd been left with enough money to buy some stability, although we were burning through it with foolish impulsivity. As an only child, I'd also been left with sole responsibility for my father. It was a fate I did not want to befall my own child.

This time, it took more than a single heat of swimmers to reach the fallopian finish line. I spent a full twelve months ovulation-tracking before Sophie was conceived, also on a birthday—her sister's fifth. I was infinitely more relaxed the second time around. I had a proper paid mat-leave, and Dan had a good job in social housing. There were a couple of years of relative calm.

But, there was a very large elephant in our house. I could not keep denying that my husband had a serious substance use problem. When we'd first been together, Dan's drinking and drug use was on par with that of our peers. Even after a mortifying incident where he stole my mother's Valium out of the bathroom cabinet, mixed it with who knows what all, and spent three days of Christmas vacation stoned out of his mind, both my mother and I forgave his youthful transgression.

Unfortunately, age didn't solve anything. Codeine prescribed for Emma's cough gone, the empty bottle left in the bathroom. Tylenol 3s from my tubal ligation vanished. Bottles of vodka stashed behind books on the shelf. Dan remained functional, and was naturally animated, so it was hard to tell when he'd had a few beers too many. But he had, almost every day.

He'd done his best to step up after my mum died, but soon stopped being a spouse and became like one of the children. If someone wanted to know if he was free on Tuesday, he'd have to ask me, which drove me to distraction. There is nothing I like more than a surprise, but he did not have the inclination or wherewithal to pull one off for my birthday or our anniversary. I even had to fill my own Christmas stocking, just as my mother had done until I figured out about Santa. Dan quite often had to inquire as to the whereabouts of his pants, and the answer was quite often the top of the fridge, where he'd plop them after getting comfy and starting happy hour with a cold beer. His interest in sex with me had completely tanked; at my insistence, we'd managed it twice between Sophie's arrival and her fourth birthday, when I called it quits.

Many times, I told Dan I needed more from him, and that I wanted him to do something about his drinking. I didn't have the courage to call it his addiction. He repeatedly promised he would. Eventually, with nothing changed, I told him I wanted us to separate. We broke it to the girls together after dinner one night. Dan was going to move to a little flat on the top floor of a nearby house, an apartment that had provided temporary accommodation for a series of newly single dads from our school, as it happened. We all four had a cry, then we went into the family room and watched an episode of *Dharma and Greg*. A week or two later, on moving day, a small van arrived. Dan hadn't packed and had to run around grabbing personal items. The next day, we met for breakfast at Golden Griddle, as if we were friends. At thirty-three, when most people are just settling down, I was done being married and having babies.

Cinderella's in a Meeting

WITH YOUR FIRST KID, you can get away with pretending there are only public education channels on TV. You can dress them however you want, providing you can tolerate people's assumptions about their gender. But once they go to school or daycare, the princess barrage begins. It wasn't as bad thirty years ago as it is now, but Emma developed an instant fondness for dresses and Disney as soon as she was exposed to them. I must have rented *Cinderella* from Blockbuster twenty-five times but would not break down and buy it. And then along came Barbie. Resistance was futile.

The longer I held out, the more alluring Barbie became. Her father and I eventually relented, but we compromised—if Emma was going to get a doll with missile-shaped boobs and a midsection so small it wouldn't fit the usual human organs, it wasn't going to be blond and blue-eyed as well. We got her a Black Barbie. She was thrilled to bits. She played for hours with this doll and a growing collection of additional Barbies, and there was much of the usual outfit-changing involved. But after a few years, Emma and her little friend Jennifer got tired of the constraints of this traditional style of play and made up a new game: they hurled their Barbies at the wall to make their heads and limbs fly off. First player with just a torso wins. Then they'd hold elaborate funerals, using a wooden wine box for a coffin.

Smitten as she was with the movie, Emma liked to play-act Cinderella. One day she cast her dad and me as the ugly stepsisters. "Ugly" is a problematic qualifier, but these are two of the juicier roles in the story. Emma wanted to play the controlling stepmother, which kind of made me happy. To me, there is nothing better than a "bossy" five-year-old girl.

"What about Cinderella?" I asked.

Without missing a beat, Emma answered, "Oh, she's at a meeting."

I was glad to know her indoctrination into princess culture was patchy at best.

⚬

Emma and Sophie went to alternative schools that were supposed to be all equity, sweetness, and light, but misogyny makes its way into the corridors of elementary school as insidiously as all corridors of power. Having shaken off her earlier primary school timidity, Emma was a girl who strode purposefully down the hall and spoke her mind. Arguing some point with a boy in her Grade 9 class, she was called "butch," meant very much as an insult. It worked—briefly. She was so taken aback, she initially tried to "correct" whatever unfeminine behaviour this boy equated with having an opinion. Now over thirty, she still catches herself trying to please and placate—a trait shared by many people whose parents had substance use disorders. Emma happens to be tall and blond and is well aware of the advantages she enjoys as a result. Fortunately, she uses her power for good, and when she walks through doors that open automatically for her, she holds them open for others.

Homophobia was also everywhere, though subtler at Emma's arts high school than most places, since the male population was disproportionately gay. She had a gay mother, and a gay first boyfriend (I knew it at the time, they found out later). When she'd hear "gay" used as a slur in the most ridiculous of contexts, she would make a point of countering, "Oh, do you mean that cardigan enjoys the company of other brown sweaters?"

About a month into her first year of university on the east coast, she called to thank me for raising her in a world without Tories. It wasn't that I'd sheltered her from right-wingers, but we'd just never moved in those circles and we had virtually no relatives, redneck or otherwise. She'd met a gay student from the prairies whose parents had kicked him out of the house as soon as he came out (or was found out) and were not supporting him in any way. He didn't last the term, poor kid.

Emma had won herself a full scholarship to university. If I believed in karma, I might recount it this way: In 2002, I worked for an excellent small agency serving homeless and marginalized youth. We delivered a program combining popular theatre, life skills, job skills, and counselling. We were running out of money, due to a hard-right turn in government, so I sold my car and used the proceeds to fund the last few weeks of the final session. I was the executive director, and felt a responsibility to the staff, and to a group of participants who'd pretty much been shat on their whole lives. Giving up my cute little Volkswagen was nothing compared to what these kids had been through. Nobody really needs a car in the city, and the insurance was costing me an arm and a leg. The following tax year, Revenue Canada gave me a hefty refund, thanks to that charitable donation, which I used to send Emma on a course in Europe for the summer. She deserved it, after the events of that winter and spring.

She couldn't leave with the rest of the Ontario kids because her father had just died, the night before her scheduled departure, but she still wanted to go. Needed to. Arrangements were made for her to catch up with the group in Paris four days late. She left directly from the small funeral we held. She turned seventeen in Prague and won an award at the end of the course for being the most engaged student. A year later, she wrote about her difficult decision to take that trip in an essay that got her short-listed for the most generous scholarship in Canada. When she received it, she gave me back the meagre savings I'd amassed for her education. The ripple effect of that one gesture—to donate the proceeds from my car— was enormous. Not that I believe in karma.

Like a great many mothers, I had always resented that I was "Duty Mum" while the girls' father got to be "Goofball Dad." But I've come to realize that my daughters saw me as someone they could count on to get shit done, and that's who they became as well, on their own behalf and in solidarity with others.

Free Fall

I LEFT MY MARRIAGE in my early thirties, after thirteen years of domesticity. Having failed to sow my wild oats at the appropriate time, I found myself enjoying very satisfying sex with an attractive older man within weeks of my separation. I met him in a stand-up comedy class; I was a student, he was the instructor. Our intense mutual attraction was an ego-boost and a welcome distraction to both of us. A couple of years later, when I started dating women, Dan conveniently changed the narrative of our breakup into my coming out story, but that wasn't it.

Avi, my new lover, was going through his second divorce, and had his own small children. We agreed that our grown-up life would not cross over into our family lives and vice versa. It was also understood that this relationship would never lead to marriage, because I was not Jewish—a prerequisite for becoming wife number three. I was mostly happy with this arrangement, which surprised me; I'd always thought I needed love and commitment in combination with sex.

My new relationship sent Dan into a tizzy, though it seemed a given that we were free to see other people. We were back under the same roof, on different floors, trying not very successfully to keep things consistent for the girls. Dan hadn't been able to do any real parenting from his small bachelor pad. He had quit his job and was not bringing in any money as a "consultant." He was living on the proceeds from my buyout of his share of the house, which was small, given that he'd contributed no capital to its purchase.

He also wanted to believe I'd come to my senses and reconfigure the furniture and the family into one household again. Soon after I started dating Avi, Dan had his first drunk driving incident, but wasn't caught. He blamed it on me, for upsetting him. One night, he backed me into a corner of my bedroom and started shouting at me, inches from my face, "What do you think you're doing? Sleeping around five seconds after we separate? Don't you care what you're doing to the girls?" He was a big man, and I was shaken. We'd never so much as raised our voices with each other, though perhaps we should have. When I told Avi about it, he asked if Dan had hit me. Although I'd felt threatened, I was shocked that he would suggest such a thing. We were feminists. We were pacifists. Luckily, it didn't happen again.

My relationship with Avi was intense but ultimately time-limited. After a couple of years, it had run its course, and devolved into a friends-with-benefits situation. Avi died in a car crash not long after we'd settled into a warm platonic friendship. When I got the news, I was devastated. Avi had given me new life as a sexual being, and suddenly his life was over.

Dan eventually met someone lovely, and I kept letting my daughters spend alternate weeks at the house he shared with her. It was the modern thing to do. Dan's girlfriend, Molly, took good care of them, but my pain was acute when they weren't with me. I distracted myself with hard work and extracurricular sex and romance. I had moved on to another sultry affair, this time with a married man. Given the circumstances, this was not an exclusive arrangement, so I took the opportunity, at long last, to explore my homosexual desire. For a couple of tantalizing years, I dated both men and women, one of each on a particularly memorable day. After my final fling with a man drew to a close, I just didn't feel inspired to seek out men anymore, and quite seamlessly came to identify as a lesbian.

Meanwhile, the grip of Dan's addiction was becoming increasingly firm. There was an acutely embarrassing incident the day of Emma's Grade 6 graduation. He'd volunteered to provide snacks but arrived late and tipsy with a woefully inadequate bag of fruit. The evil stares of the mothers in charge sent him straight back out, not to a grocery store, but to a bar. He returned pissed to the gills just in time for the ceremony. In his absence, the mums had cobbled together a buffet of refreshments. One snipped to me, "I could kill your ex-husband!" I said, "Take a number."

There were more impaired driving incidents until Dan lost his license. Drunk cycling, he at least couldn't do much harm to others. One night, he took a fall down the stairs and seriously injured his shoulder. The girls and I visited the next day. Molly was fashioning a sling for him in their kitchen. His hands were shaking uncontrollably. He looked at me, a deer caught in the headlights, and said, "It's because of the pain." I was the one person who wouldn't pretend that was true, but I didn't call him out on it in such a vulnerable state in front of the girls. He went to the hospital and was admitted for surgery, but had a mild heart attack caused by withdrawal before he got to the operating table. Only then did the gravity of his situation become undeniable to everyone.

His rapid downward spiral came as no surprise to me, but that didn't make it any easier to watch. I was prepared for the worst, and so was Emma, thanks to an astute therapist. I had taken custody of Sophie when she was nine, since she was no longer safe in her father's care. Emma was old enough by that point to make her own choices and tried spending time with her dad for a while, but stopped visiting altogether after his dramatic hospitalization.

Not infrequently, when the girls were due for a weekend visit, we'd round the corner onto Dan's street to find

Molly signalling from the porch that he was in no state to receive them. I'd keep driving, sometimes to one of the restaurants on Roncesvalles that the girls liked, in an effort to salvage our Friday night. I did a bang-up job of teaching them to eat their feelings. Wood-fired pizza in lieu of fiery rage.

Molly made a final ultimatum—go to rehab or leave. Her deadline came and went, and Dan went on a bender, crashing around inside their house like a raccoon trapped in a shed. He had to be removed by the cops. He was involuntarily committed to hospital for the allowable seventy-two hours. During that time, Emma and I cleared the last of the girls' belongings from Molly's house. Sophie was away in Algonquin Park at a sleepover camp, and I was glad she didn't have to participate in this glum transfer of goods. We wrapped up late afternoon on July first. I remember the date, because we rode our bikes down to the waterfront to watch the Canada Day fireworks that night, to distract ourselves.

Dan was discharged to make his own way to an available bed at the Salvation Army's rehab program. He arrived there, but they told him he was missing a necessary form and would have to return to the hospital to obtain it. It was pushing forty degrees with Toronto's infamous humidex that day, and he didn't even have subway fare. He left. Nobody heard from him all day. I got a call from him in the early evening but missed it. He left a message that said, "No kind of service." That was all. I understood it immediately—he didn't want a funeral. I had no idea where he was. Family members were downtown looking for him, but Toronto is a very big place. We had all agreed not to take him in, so he would understand that the closest people in his life were united with Molly in insisting that he go to rehab.

Molly found him in her backyard the next morning. He'd slept there, after a very cordial evening with friends, to whom he had revealed nothing of his situation. He asked to come in to use the phone and computer. He called his previous night's host to say thank you for a lovely dinner. He called my house. I was so relieved. He asked to speak to Emma. It was early and she was sound asleep. I asked if he could call a bit later. I didn't ask if he'd thought better of killing himself. He sounded good, and I remember being afraid to remind him, to spook him somehow. I was hoping he might have been too drunk to remember leaving a message on my machine. He said he wasn't sure if he'd be able to call later, and I thought he meant he was going to rehab, where there might only be a public payphone. Emma was very grumpy about being woken. She was due to leave the next day for the month-long study tour in Europe that I'd paid for with my tax refund. I really thought she needed some fun, far from home. Dan wanted to say good-bye.

A short while later, I talked to Molly, who said Dan had wanted to pull his résumé and some other job search files from the computer, which sounded promising. She had given him a subway token to get back to the Sally Ann.

People in step programs are encouraged to face the reality that they have three stark choices: recovery, jail, or death. Dan picked a bridge. The police went to his mother's house around dinnertime. She phoned Molly and me. Molly came over with her brother who had arrived in town to help prepare her house for roommates. We went to the toy store where Emma worked part-time. I called her manager first, so I could rush her out without explanation. I knew she'd know what had happened as soon as she saw me. She was in tears the minute we got out the door.

We convened at the home of a relative, where it was agonizingly awkward and some family members were trying to cast blame on the hospital, or the Salvation Army, or themselves. But I knew—and so did Emma—that the details didn't matter. If it hadn't been that day, it would have been a different day. Dan was not going to choose recovery. We could grieve, but ultimately we had to live with his decision.

Molly's brother drove us to Algonquin Park the next day, where Sophie's camp director was waiting to take us by boat to the island where she was staying. He whisked us to a private cabin. Sophie had just come from a swim and was chatting with a camp counsellor as she climbed, dripping wet, up a small hill from the lake. She also knew as soon as she saw us.

We did have a service, because they are for the living, of course. There was a certain amount of confusion because Dan had not updated his Will since our separation, so I had to sign off on various things as exec-utor. I remember running around the neighbourhood before we drove north to get Sophie, trying to find a fax machine so I could give the undertaker permission to let his mother make decisions regarding his remains. I also ended up arranging for a close friend of Dan's to offici-ate a kind of DIY service at the cemetery, where his ashes were buried in his father's plot. I wrote a eulogy, the gist of which was that Dan had done what he felt he must, to stop hurting himself and the people he loved. I didn't know the half of it.

I phoned my dad the morning after Dan died to tell him the news. I was supposed to rent a car that day to take Emma to the airport and then to drive him to do some-thing or other. He said, "So Dan's killed himself, but you should still get the car to do your errands." I explained very briefly about what was happening—going to get Sophie, Emma delaying her departure to Europe—but he just kept repeating instructions about renting a car. It was the best he could do. He'd survived countless suicide attempts, starting when I was eleven. Sophie was eleven. The irony could not have been lost on him.

Take Back the Night

I WAS TWENTY-THREE years old and had just given birth to my first child. One night, pacing frantically back and forth with my wailing newborn strapped to my chest, I discovered that I was, at the very minimum, bisexual. And it was all because of Robert Palmer.

MuchMusic (now known as Much) was new, and I had the television on in the background while I wore a path in the carpet. The iconic music video for "Addicted to Love" came on, featuring Palmer's signature backup "band" of models with shiny red lips, slicked-back hair, and micro-skirts. It's quite dreadful, really—all those glassy-eyed women fake-playing guitars. I was recovering from an infected episiotomy, yet somehow, in my sleep-deprived postpartum state, I was wildly turned on by them. I thought, "Huh," and filed the incident away.

My mother had always been my grounding force.

She was a scientist and an artist, a pragmatist and a creator. Her death when I was twenty-six left me with only my young husband to lean on, and he was not a solid structure. My intense grief coincided with two conflicting impulses: I decided I wanted another baby; and I fell in love with a woman. Dan had lost interest in sex, probably because he was drinking heavily by this time. This impeded the first situation and facilitated the latter. But having just been through the agony of dealing with one terminally ill and one mentally ill parent with no siblings to share the load, I was determined that Emma should not be an only child.

My professional circle in the not-for-profit sector was disproportionately full of out lesbians, closeted lesbians, and women who, like me, were curious and would later make a full switch. During my mother's illness, I had gravitated toward my coworker Joan, who could not have looked more butch, but was married to a man. I obsessed about her and directed much unsolicited attention her way. Six months after my mum's death, although I was diligently forcing myself on Dan on ovulation days, I professed my love to her at a Take Back the Night march. I had no clear intentions, just a fantasy in which we absconded from real life to raise babies together. She gently indicated that she didn't want to leave her marriage (yet...she did come out later), nor did she want to have an affair. It was too uncomfortable to be around her, so I left that job. Immediately upon starting a new one, I got pregnant.

I felt it only fair to tell Dan about my attraction to Joan. He had never been the jealous type and was remarkably unperturbed. He dismissed my feelings as a reaction to the void left by my mother. He was onboard with having another child. He loved our first daughter with all his heart, and was a hands-on, diaper-changing dad.

After I left him, I dated men for another few years, then I took the plunge and asked out another mum at Sophie's school. Chatter quickly spread among the parents, which struck me as odd. It was a liberal alternative school, and by then Ellen had come out on TV, and *Will and Grace* was a prime-time hit. It was uncomfortable to be the object of so much attention. I remember another mother saying to me in a hushed voice, "I saw your 'friend' in the paper," referring to a front-page picture from the Dyke March. She seemed to be going for a wink-wink-nudge-nudge tone but couldn't manage the word "girlfriend." Even Dan didn't like it when he overheard one mother say to another, "There's nothing *wrong* with it, but I didn't want to have to introduce the subject so soon." As if the mind-boggling mechanics of heterosexuality require no explanation to a child!

I preferred to keep my adult adventures to myself, but Emma had picked up a suggestive message from my lover on the answering machine, and another Grade 2 kid had told Sophie that her mummy was dating Janie's mummy. Neither of my daughters batted an eye. Dan opportunistically ventured the opinion that I was adding to the girls' burden as children of a broken home, but he didn't really buy into what he was saying, and sheepishly let it drop. We had raised our children to be ambassadors for inclusion, and they had other preoccupations. If asked, they would probably have said that the most interesting thing to happen in our family in 1999 was that we got a dog.

After my initial foray into lesbian life (the other mum was firmly polyamorous, which wasn't really my cup of tea), I had another quick fling with a married former colleague, whose husband seemed to feel that sex with a woman didn't count as infidelity and was probably titillated by the whole thing. For him, sex revolved around the almighty penis. But not for me. By that time, I was in hot pursuit of the alternative.

Online dating had become the new normal, so I tried my luck on a site called The Pink Sofa. I had just started seeing someone I'd met in cyberspace when another suitor appeared out of the blue. As it turned out, our meeting was not coincidental, but in fact orchestrated down to the very last detail. A mutual acquaintance had arranged for Kate to attend a feminist event that I helped organize and had fed her as much biographical information as was available. Oblivious, I brought my Pink Sofa lady, confounding everyone who was in on the scheme.

Undaunted, Kate took several opportunities to flirt, sidling up to me at the chocolate fountain and suggestively immersing pieces of fruit. She made an awkward joke about bananas being too phallic for the occasion. Once the dignitaries were gone, I unwound by dancing with some spritely young grassroots activists, inadvertently affording Kate a clear view down my blouse. The next day, our matchmaker was more forthright in her meddling, asking me if she could give Kate my phone number. It was all very flattering.

We had brunch the following weekend. Kate had a second activity up her sleeve, in the hope we'd want to extend our date. She took me to a flea market at a hipster hotel—a fundraiser for the Inside Out LGBT film festival. It was a treasure trove of books, which I kept holding up for Kate to see as I added to my pile. "Have you read this?" I'd ask. "Don't you love Jane Urquhart?" She mumbled something and wandered off toward the used biker boots. It turned out Kate had not picked up a book since university and never read for pleasure.

I did not run the opposite way, library card clutched to my bosom. Instead, I shook myself free of the other woman I'd been seeing, and Kate and I willingly embodied the classic joke, "What does a lesbian bring on a second date? A U-Haul." I was smug, so sure that at the advanced age of forty-four, I could distinguish love from lust. I convinced myself that house-hunting with someone after four months together was a perfectly rational thing to be doing. In truth, I was ignoring ample evidence to suggest we had nothing in common, stumbling along in a constant post-coital haze. Our lovemaking was affirming and unrestrained, and I was giddy.

I saw no comparison to my first illogical leap into domestic partnership two decades earlier. I felt utterly comfortable with Kate. We fit together, and we laughed. I experienced a small flutter of joy when her car pulled into the driveway. After so much solitude and plain hard work, I relished our weekend ritual of tea and coffee in bed. Our politics were aligned, so we had plenty to say to each other about LGBT issues, workers' rights, racism, women's equality. We just avoided the majority of topics which held no interest for one or the other of us. Kate had been a star athlete until an injury ended her promising sports career. I had been the kid with an inhaler and excellent grammar.

My daughters thought I was being ridiculous, of course, but were happy for me. I had let them make their own mistakes, and they granted me the same courtesy. For a while, it seemed pleasant enough at our house, though Kate and fifteen-year-old Sophie rarely spent time alone together or interacted. At dinner, they both directed their conversation toward me. We had lots of space, so if I was out teaching at night, they'd more than likely be watching separate TVs on different floors.

In our bedroom, which we'd merrily painted a colour called "lavender lipstick," we continued to experiment unabashedly and to satisfy each other in ways neither of us had enjoyed before. I'd always loved sex and orgasmed with minimal persuasion. My last male lover, whom I'd been seeing while also sleeping with a woman for the first time, jokingly lamented that by defecting to the other team, I was taking away my gift to the male ego. I figured the male ego would manage without me.

My work had become ever more precarious. I had an unerring ability to choose jobs dependent on government funding that would dry up with the next political shift. After yet another layoff, I decided I'd fulfill a fantasy and open my own retail arts business. To facilitate this financially, we rented out the basement of our house, meaning that Sophie had to share much closer quarters with us. She and Kate began to grate on each other. Kate had no patience for Sophie's snippiness and self-absorption. I remembered myself as a teenager and thought we were getting off easy.

Around Sophie's eighteenth birthday, Kate started to make noises about not being able to live with her, and I became uncharacteristically passive, afraid of losing my relationship, afraid of loneliness. It was such a welcome relief to share the burden of being an adult with someone. Sophie got the message and moved out, though she had not quite finished high school. She put on a brave face and went along with my rationalizing list of benefits to independent living but felt forced out of her own home.

Kate had a condo picked out before Sophie's books were even packed, and I numbly agreed to move into it with her. I didn't even like it. It was in a fancy concrete box full of old people. Emma joked that we had gone beyond Lesbian U-Haul Syndrome and were suffering from full-blown Lesbian U-Haul Chronic Disorder. I chose to keep only a quarter stake in our communal property, freeing up more cash for my fledgling enterprise. Sophie seemed okay in her shared digs nearby, and I went back to the comforts of hot sex and hot dinners, both waiting for me after a long day at my shop. Just as I had with Dan, I let myself be soothed by a nice roast chicken.

Sophie and I had it out after a weekend when she'd been cat-sitting. She did not spare my feelings in letting me know how much I'd hurt her by putting Kate first. We cried and yelled and hugged and cried some more, and I apologized for my unconscionable maternal offence. That was what she needed—acknowledgement that I'd fucked up badly. At the same time, she had the generosity to acknowledge how hard it must have been for me as the only competent parent, and then the only parent, of two headstrong girls who'd suffered severe trauma. She quite liked living on her own, but I made sure we saw more of each other after that.

Kate never joined Sophie and me on our excursions, but she made the sweet gesture of flying Emma in from Halifax for my birthday, about ten months after we'd moved into "Club Crone" (my name for our empty nest). I was delighted to have my daughters together, and the three of us spent a week playing Scrabble and taking in art. Meanwhile, Kate stewed because her space had been invaded, and because I was so noticeably enjoying activities she disliked.

Emma went back east to university, and Kate became sullen, barely moving from the couch when she got home from work. She wouldn't open up to me, insisting she had to work through her own shit. I tried to let her be. She was still physically affectionate, although we were rarely making love anymore. A few times I brought up the obvious issue that my children were never going to go away, suggesting we see a counsellor to help us resolve it.

My guess is that Kate had assumed she'd have me all to herself the minute my children turned eighteen, perhaps because she'd distanced herself from her own parents as an adult. She was surprised when Sophie took a three-hour bus trip to join us for her mother's funeral. Either she didn't recognize this was what families do, or she didn't recognize that we were a family. She was in the habit of making what she called "stay in the will" visits once or twice a year and hadn't even come out to her family until after we were living together, and then only because she couldn't sustain the web of lies surrounding her change of address.

The truth was forced out of her during a conversation with her parents, each on separate phone extensions. Her dad asked for utilitarian details about our newly acquired property—the furnace, the garage, the roof. She'd told them she was moving in with a friend, closer to her work. I could hear Kate telling him about the layout, explaining that my daughter had her own sitting room and bedroom in the basement.

Suddenly her mum chimed in, "Do you have your own bedroom?"

"No," said Kate after a deep breath. "I share a bedroom with Mary."

"Well, do you have your own bed?" her mum asked mischievously.

"No, Mum," said Kate at long last. "We share a bed. We're a couple."

After a pause, her dad broke the tension: "Well, do you have your own study?"

"Yes!" said Kate. "I do have my own study!"

"Well, that's nice," said her dad.

Soon after this momentous exchange, her mother's Alzheimer's rapidly worsened, which meant that Kate had to come out all over again, every time we saw her, and sometimes several times within the same conversation.

"Katie, honey, do you think you'll ever get married again?"

"Mum, this is my partner, Mary, remember?"

"Oh yes, dear, is my Katie nice to you?"

"Yes, Betsy, she's very nice."

"Katie, dear, the doctor here is single and quite handsome."

"Mum, remember Mary, my partner? We live together."

"Oh, yes, of course. Do you girls like dancing?"

Nobody would have confused Kate for a straight person, not even in the photo of her at four years old, looking miserable in an itchy wool dress, forlornly holding a softball in one hand. We found Kate's wedding album at the family cottage. Inside were pictures of a small-town lesbian and gay man doing what they thought they must. On the outside, in her mother's writing, was a label that read, "Katie and Carl, 1985—." Even on their wedding day, she was well aware that union had an expiration date.

I had not come out to my own parents, either, but this was mostly a matter of timing. The incident involving the Robert Palmer video had hardly seemed newsworthy, so I hadn't mentioned it to my mother. My father wouldn't have dreamed of asking me whether I was dating or interested in marrying again. He stuck to the short list of topics he could handle: watches, dogs, cars, and items found in the L.L. Bean catalogue, for which he had developed a peculiar attachment. Kate and I met the spring after he died. I would have told him about her, introducing tidbits of information in tiny, digestible portions. He had learned not to call grown women "girls" after many decades of reinforcement. I expect he would have come to accept that being queer was fine.

One Saturday morning, as I was getting ready for work, Kate announced that she couldn't stay around and was going out of town for the weekend. I attributed this to Sophie's presence in our spare room, where she was spending a couple of weeks before heading abroad. But the desperation in Kate's tone scared me. I asked a question I was sure she'd answer with a resounding, "No!" Did she want me to move out? She answered, "Yes...but I don't want you to lose the shop." Those would be the last words we ever spoke in person to each other.

I found an apartment that very day. I was stunned and couldn't stop crying; I had called in my part-time employee to cover the shop. Sophie kindly came with me and instructed me to sign the lease. We now shared the experience of eviction by the same woman. Kate couch-surfed for a couple of weeks until Sophie and I had cleared out. In a small but satisfying gesture of pettiness, I got our collection of sex toys from its discreet location, took the incomparable Hitachi wand for myself, and strewed the rest around under the bed, hoping that on Kate's moving day, some burly guys would lift the box spring and laugh to find them there. A month later, I also snuck into our little patio garden and ate every last cherry tomato we had planted together.

I passed quickly from the shock of being blindsided to the mortification of having been blindsided. I had clued in to the fact that my relationship was in trouble at the eleventh hour but had never expected to be thrown out like a used Kleenex.

With such a small share in our property, and no further access to credit, I really was at risk of losing my business, which I loved, and had vowed to give a fighting chance. Kate and I had to communicate regarding the division of assets and sale of Club Crone. I sent some emails—furious at first but increasingly rational in tone—proposing what I thought would be fair. The next thing I knew, I received a letter from a lawyer, telling me that communication with his client should henceforth go through him.

My sadness turned to rage. I can't abide rudeness. My mother, like her mother before her, instilled in me a deep appreciation for good manners; hearing from someone's lawyer is just not called for. Although I had daily conversations with Kate in my head for a full year, they were not laments for lost love, but rather diatribes about proper breakup etiquette. I adopted Sophie's pet name for her: DevilHornMcPoopFace.

I reached out after a year to ask if we could talk. I would have liked an explanation, since I'd been left to draw my own conclusions. But all I got back was a text that sounded like it was drafted by either her lawyer or her therapist: "I don't think it is in my interest to communicate with you." From U-Hauling to playing an annual round of Dodge-the-Ex at Pride...my first major same-sex love affair ended as it had begun—with a cliché.

Do You Believe in God?

'

I USED TO HALF-JOKE that if Sophie had been born before Emma, she'd have been an only child. Even in utero, she was a handful, calling out the midwives for sustained bouts of contractions on several occasions over a three-week period, before finally bursting onto the scene in a ninety-minute whirlwind of agony and ecstasy. She was an utterly charming baby but tolerated no bullshit from the outset. Her sister had been content with milk from a boob or a bottle, providing it was made available in a timely manner, but this little one screwed up her face in outrage when we proffered a silicone nipple, as if to say, "What kind of a fool do you take me for?" Her whole first year, I had to arrange my work and life to keep the dairy bar open for her twenty-four hours a day.

As soon as she learned to talk, it was like tuning in to Toddler Radio all day long. In the tub, she would make up long, bewitching stories involving a large cast of characters: shampoo bottles, bars of soap, plastic tubs, hairbrushes, and assorted toy ducks and boats. I'd have to keep adding hot water because she wouldn't get out until the plot reached its dénouement.

By two, Sophie was an emotional hurricane, nearly tearing the roof off buildings. She would experience fits of frustration, often because she couldn't do all the clever, coordinated things her eight-year-old sister could do. For whatever reason, her tantrums tended to involve stripping off her clothes. Sustained naked screaming on the floor would ensue. On winter days, I sometimes had to ask a friend with a car to collect us from daycare to get my bare-skinned child safely home in the bitter cold.

One evening when Sophie was in kindergarten, I got a call from another mother who'd chaperoned a field trip that day. She wanted to let me know that Sophie had pestered her all the way home on the school bus about matters of a spiritual nature. The woman was more astonished than offended. Sophie had wanted to know, "Do you believe in God? Why? What do you think God is like?" My parents hadn't baptized me, reasoning that they couldn't possibly know what beliefs I'd ascribe to later in life. My kids were raised devoutly atheist. But Sophie wasn't going to take her parents' word for anything without further scrutiny.

By the time Sophie was six or seven, her tantrums had evolved into junior panic attacks, and my therapist recommended a colleague who specialized in art therapy for children. She met with Sophie a few times, and then asked to meet with Dan and me individually. In short order, she'd identified Dan's unreliable caregiving as part of the problem and called him in to address his own issues. She told me that since Dan's life was so chaotic, I had to be consistently strong for Sophie. Not to show uncertainty or weakness. Not to crumple. Sophie would often complain that I was unmovable and unapologetic. I was constantly torn between being a regular vulnerable person and being her rock, between coming down hard on Dan and giving him room to be a co-parent. I couldn't get it right.

Dan was self-medicating heavily, resisting professional treatment for depression and addiction. He saw in Sophie the melancholy he tended to romanticize in himself. She was so bloody smart; she could spot injustice and hypocrisy a mile away. It hurt her when kids were mean, and when adults were insincere. Instead of consoling her and reassuring her of the goodness of people, Dan confirmed her suspicion that the world was, in fact, a cold, uncaring place. It was as if he wanted an ally in his misery—someone to support his contention that the universe owed him something. It was impossible for me to know what he was feeding her, because we had shared custody and the girls split their time between us. Dan easily convinced Sophie that her therapist was full of shit, so she wouldn't want to go anymore. I did not yet have the confidence to fight back.

Sophie was not a kid who could keep her brains to herself—not even to fit in. Emma was gregarious, got along with everyone, and had a huge posse of friends. She quite often kept her hand down in class, even when she knew the answer. Sophie was more like I had been as a child, seeking closeness with just a couple of kindred spirits. She was given advanced schoolwork to keep her mind occupied, which never goes over well with one's peers. It was simple for the powerful girls in her Grade 4 class to isolate her from the herd. One of them invented a club to which everyone could belong except "tinkers," a word she chose at random to mean smarty-pants girls. To mean Sophie. This nine-year-old ringleader wouldn't have known that this word can also be used to describe menders and wanderers, often refugees.

It was the new millennium and the correct term for this age-old behaviour was bullying. Adults intervened, but the damage was done. Sophie refused to attend school. Her truancy catapulted her to the head of the queue for special ed testing, and a spot was secured for her at a school with a gifted stream that she could join in the new term. Meanwhile, she came to work with me at an agency for homeless and marginalized youth. She helped the cook prepare lunch and read books in my office. But she was hurting, and her prodigious vocabulary couldn't help her say what was going on. She had internalized her dad's pain and taken on the task of saving him.

She started hurting herself, not seriously, but scarily. At the tender age of nine, she was experiencing suicidal thoughts. She was acting out her rage and pain, as I had done, but precociously early. She kept trying to get her hands on knives at her dad's house, which had to be swept for sharps. There was one ambulance trip when we could not get Sophie to calm down, and another ER visit which got us nowhere. So, we took her to see the doctor Dan had chosen to replace her previous therapist. I had no idea this one was a family doctor posing as a psychiatrist/psycho-therapist, for which she was later censured by her medical governing body. I had gone along with Dan's selection to get his buy-in, so that he wouldn't sabotage Sophie's treatment again. He was in such a state by this time that he was prepared to sacrifice her well-being to avoid facing his addiction and the injuries he was inflicting on his whole family. The doctor called over to the hospital to say Sophie was having psychotic episodes (she wasn't) and had her admitted for a week. The nurses assured me she did not belong in hospital. On the day she was released, Dan very effectively underlined the point Sophie had been trying to make.

He arrived so wasted, the staff would not let Sophie get in his car. One of the social workers phoned me but assured me he would see the pair of them into a cab. The hospital performed its due diligence by contacting the Children's Aid Society, but inexplicably abdicated respon-sibility for Sophie's safety by letting her leave with Dan at all. And I didn't jump in and insist they wait for me to arrive. Instead, I sat bawling in my living room for an hour. Meanwhile, Dan had instructed the cabbie to drive him to his car in the parking lot and had sent Sophie off alone in the taxi.

She arrived safely at my door, very glad to be home and quite chipper, though disappointed she hadn't been able to give her dad the special wreath she'd made him in occupational therapy. A few minutes later, I saw Dan pull up outside my house and sent Emma and Sophie upstairs to watch TV. When I replay this scene in my mind, I somehow grab his car keys and call the police. In reality, I blocked him from entering and called his partner Molly to tell her he was on his way. Miraculously, he didn't crash into anything until he got to his own driveway, then banged up the car trying to insert it into the garage. He was so far gone on a combination of pills and booze, Molly had to get backup to contain him until he sobered up more than twenty-four hours later.

A child protection worker phoned me the next day. She asked me all kinds of necessarily invasive questions about my own lifestyle and parenting and the girls' activities and routines. After ten minutes, she seemed satisfied that Sophie had one responsible parent, and was pretty much ready to close the file, but made a visit to Dan's later that week to complete her report. He turned the contrition up to top volume. Emma underplayed the impact of his behaviour. Sophie recalled lying through her teeth.

I started proceedings to take custody of Sophie and Dan offered no objection. Sophie was visibly relieved. Should I have done it much sooner? In retrospect, the answer seems obvious, but at the time, I was afraid of alienating everyone, including my daughters, with unpredictable fallout. A few attempts to solicit help for Dan were met with hostility from family and friends, who found him charming and had the impression he was a super-dad. I was alone and stuck.

Dan had always read to the girls and sung them to sleep when they were little, as did I. As they grew older, he continued to go into their rooms for a cuddle, as did I. Some of our best mother-daughter talks would happen in those moments. But Dan would inevitably be drunk or stoned or both, which made him maudlin. Emma has told me—recently, as we try to unravel the snarled tangles of the past—that he'd pass out, and then she and Molly would have to rouse him and lug him to his own bed.

Sophie put a stop to these bedtime visits; Dan then punished her by convincing her that she wasn't very bright—he hit where he would do the most damage, since Sophie's intellect was her most prized possession. Her IQ had tested through the roof, but she got the message. By her early teens, she reasoned that if she didn't have superior smarts to protect, she might as well fry her brain with some soothing drugs. Dan was seriously fucked up by this point, unrecognizable from the man I'd married. And he seemed hell-bent on taking Sophie down with him.

Dan and I had never bothered to divorce, so the custody process involved formalizing our responsibilities. We had more or less shared expenses, though I had often received calls from the girls' music teachers and summer camps to say they hadn't been paid or Dan's cheque had bounced. Every time, I would cover for him so the girls wouldn't find out or have to withdraw from their activities.

My lawyer wrote up a divorce and custody agreement including child support. Dan signed, but didn't pay, so she drafted a new document allowing for his wages to be garnisheed. This he also signed without a fuss. But on the date it was supposed to take effect, he went to work drunk and got himself fired. When he died, he left no insurance and no equity in the house he shared with Molly. Strangely, when a relative said to me at his memorial, "I bet he was behind in his child support," I thought, "Why would you say that?" I had an easier time dealing with the truth about his addiction than dealing with the possibility that he wasn't really a feminist.

Sophie was relatively comfortable in her gifted class through to the end of elementary school. She'd found her people. She was bored silly when she returned to a mainstream academic classroom for high school—a trade-off for being in a performing arts program. She started smoking pot. A lot of pot. I didn't really think marijuana was such a terrible choice, as teenage risk-taking goes. I had smoked some weed in my day, and easily given it up along with other youthful habits. I didn't know she was regularly supplementing it with harder drugs and reaching a point where she couldn't get through the day without it. She was an extremely high-functioning user; her marks didn't suffer and she held down part-time jobs where she had considerable responsibility, even managing an espresso joint the summer she was seventeen. She was a superb actress, inside and outside of her drama program.

In fact, she floored me with a performance of a

one-woman play written and directed by other students in her Grade 10 class. It was a devastating story about a girl's revenge on her abusive father, and I was chilled by her portrayal of this damaged and complex character. I should have been more worried about where she dredged those emotions from.

Sophie had been looking forward to university all through the dog days of high school, but when she finally got there, anxiety set in and cost her the first term. She laid siege to her second term with sheer determination and marched on through the summer session to catch up. That July, 2013, marked the tenth anniversary of her father's suicide. In the fall, bouts of depression and surges of panic attacked her mercilessly. Shortly before Christmas, she raised the white flag. A doctor on campus sent her to hospital on a Form One, as a strategy to get her some real help rather than a speedy exit from the emergency room with a prescription for benzos. They made her go in a police car, as I followed along behind. For the requisite seventy-two hours, she was in a solitary cell. While I sat with her, we were bombarded by the sounds of people in the throes of emotional torment. I had almost forgotten those sounds.

The last time Sophie saw her dad was Father's Day, 2003. Emma didn't want to go. I knew I was taking a risk by going over to his house given the spring he'd been having. The plan was for the two of us to stay for dinner. He was obviously drunk, but we went in anyway. Something about the pull of a dumb Hallmark holiday. He was attempting to make his famous clam chowder, but kept wandering aimlessly away from the stove, and repeating himself. It was awful. We had a bit of soup then quickly departed. We were still hungry, so we walked over to Mitzi's Sister on Queen Street. I had just enough change in my pocket for some sweet potato fries.

Eleven-year-old Sophie had not been able to process her dad's death, or the destruction that preceded it. It was excruciating to see it catch up with her at twenty-one, but a mercy that her PTSD didn't lurk undetected like a malignant tumour for even longer. With fierce resolve, Sophie began her journey toward recovery.

The first half of 2014 was a period of intense learning for all of us. Sophie was admitted to a mental health facility, at first, for a two-month inpatient mood disorder program. One of the first things she had to do was stop using illegal drugs. She was connected to Narcotics Anonymous (NA) on-site and gratefully accepted what they were offering. Her self-medication had been a coping strategy; once she started receiving intensive care for her underlying illnesses, she was able to restrict her drug use to only those prescribed. Not just like that, of course. That's not how addiction works. There were relapses—quite dramatic ones—that spring during the periods when she was back home. A couple of months after the mood program, she was admitted to a combined PTSD/addiction program, designed to address the reality that PTSD and addiction often go hand in hand.

It is worth noting here that programs like these are

rarely covered by public health insurance. While we love to sing the praises of universal health care in Canada, in Ontario and other parts of the country, mental health care is delivered using a two-tiered system. Your choices are often to pay or to wait years for treatment. Sophie's first stay cost five figures. It was not what you would call elective; it was lifesaving. Somehow, magically, there was a free bed available for her second stay. It was not magic, or luck, obviously. I'm convinced that a dedicated social worker, doctor, or nurse must have done some effective lobbying on Sophie's behalf behind the scenes.

For all those weeks she was an inpatient, Sophie spent her spare time in the hospital library, researching mental illness, addiction, and treatment options. While the science remains frustratingly limited, she was determined to understand whatever there was to know. She dug in, bringing her analytical powers to bear on the problem. I cheered her on as she talked about using her experience to help others in a health care career of some kind down the road.

Sophie stopped all non-sanctioned drug use for long periods of time. NA worked for her for several years, and she was able to celebrate one year "clean" and then two years "clean" with family and friends around her. Over time, she came to view drugs differently and chose a harm-reduction model over an abstinence model for herself, while respecting others' individual choices. Her language changed, from drug "abuse" to "misuse" to "use," as it became clearer to her that the vilification of certain drugs but not others is arbitrary. She became an advocate for decriminalization, since punishing people for drug use only makes things worse. She became an advocate for safe supply, since prohibition is a proven failure and only pushes people toward dangerous alternatives to regulated pharmaceuticals.

My education started with Dan's experience, but I learned from Sophie just how complicated drug addiction is. It's genetic. It's a by-product of an immoral, money-grubbing pharmaceutical industry. It's big business inside and outside of the law. It's poorly understood, highly stigmatized, and vastly undertreated. What it's not is the result of bad behaviour, any more than alcohol addiction is the result of some underage swigs from a mickey smuggled into a high school dance.

Through this extraordinarily challenging time, when Sophie was processing so much, including a great deal of anger, it was not easy to be her mother. It was agonizing to be powerless to stop her pain. It was extremely upsetting when she went through periods of cutting that left me feeling squeamish and terrified. It was especially difficult to be on the receiving end of her emotional explosions, yet I was grateful to be her safe person, just as my mum had been to me. I went to Nar-anon (for family members of drug users) and to all the free programs I could find to support me in supporting her.

Amid all the emotional intensity, I felt the undercurrent of her appreciation, but I was surprised when Sophie decided on a grand gesture to demonstrate it. She changed her name to Breen. (My kids were given their dad's last name. In the eighties and nineties, it was hard for a feminist family to know what to do about naming. Hyphenation seemed short-sighted, passing the problem on to the next generation. I wasn't especially attached to my father's name, which I had kept when I got married, and felt no imperative to pass it along.) Taking my name was Sophie's way of consciously un-choosing one family connection, for sure, but also of acknowledging our bond. She completed the paperwork in the midst of her hospital stays, going to the trouble of replacing all her IDs. She really wanted to make me happy.

Lactation Humour

I'VE ALWAYS BEEN a class-taking kind of person when I can afford it—some kind of art activity to nurture creativity when life is unbalanced. For a dutiful sort like me, there's nothing like paying for a class to make me make art. Left to my own devices, with small children, I would only have made beds and lunches. So, when Sophie was a toddler, I took a stand-up comedy class I saw featured on a local television program.

I signed up, figuring that anything I could possibly have to do in public for the rest of my born days would be a breeze in comparison to getting up onstage at a comedy club. I was dead right about that. I wasn't a particularly timid public speaker to begin with, but no challenge has ever compared to standing in front of a room full of people, most of them men and most of them sloshed, and joking about pregnancy, childbirth, and breastfeeding.

Members of my mum's family and I had always entertained each other with our wit. My mother and her sister for several years prepared tourist brochures whenever one was going to visit the other. They would type up in hilarious detail the accommodations, menus, attractions, and entertainment available to the discerning traveller. My cousin and I would get involved, noting the amenities and indoor wildlife featured at my aunt's cottage, and the cozy-but-hip quarters at my urban satellite location. We would make carbon copies and send the original tri-fold documents in the mail. I still have a few of these yellowed testaments to pure silliness.

I also learned from my mother the skill of producing excruciatingly bad poetry—the kind where the rhymes are a painful stretch (*mocha* and *soda*, for example, or *jolly* and *mouldy*). She would write these poems to accompany gifts, which she chose and wrapped with great care, often linking items thematically. As soon as I had the language skills to write badly enough, I did the same for her. Pop psychology describes the five essential ways to show love; our dominant method was definitely gift-giving. I remember one Christmas when I gave my mum five small gifts, each associated with one of the five senses, accompanied by terrible verse. For "taste," I wrapped up a *People* magazine.

Little of this poetry has survived, unfortunately. My daughters and I took it up a notch, writing groan-worthy lyrics sung to the tune of popular songs. Of these, I do have a few examples, the best was this chorus from a song

Emma composed for me shortly after she left for university. Sung to the tune of "I Will Always Love You," it goes: "And I-I-I-I-I will never do 'shrooms, and call you at 2, like other first years do."

Musical numbers of this calibre have been withstood by unsuspecting guests at weddings, birthday parties, and graduations. After doing stand-up at a real comedy club, nothing is too embarrassing for me. For my fiftieth birthday, I asked only for bad poetry. Best party ever.

The comedy class attracted a collection of oddballs, as one might expect. Some were doing it to boost their confidence, others for a lark. One fellow was over eighty and a charmer with his collection of old standards. He didn't write any original material but was given a pass. When we eventually did our sets at Yuk Yuk's, he stole the show. One woman had joined the class to meet men, but it turned out the octogenarian was her only prospect, which provided her with a wealth of material.

I wrote about what I'd recently been through with the arrival of my second child. There is plenty that is ridiculous about the whole business of making humans and keeping them alive in those first couple of years, though these topics were taboo in comedy circles at the time. I had nothing interesting to say about dicks I've known, or things I've done while plastered, so I went for it.

Breastfeeding seems an untapped (pun intended) source of merriment. Not every lactating mother experiences this, but I must have been hopped up on hormones because I was a milk producer to rival any dairy. If I was away from my baby, or she slept for more than two hours, you could watch my breasts go from a B-cup to a double-D as if via time-lapse photography. Then they would spew forth like a fountain at a splash pad on a hot summer day. If I got the timing right, I could squirt milk clear across the room. Often my breasts would let down in the shower, spilling enough warm milk to fill a mug. On my first solo foray out into the world after Emma's birth, I went to Eaton's to buy a vacuum cleaner. As I rode the escalator to the appliance floor, milk suddenly coursed like two waterslides from my chest to my crotch. Postpartum and exhausted, I had a little cry, but still found it kind of funny. So, my boobs became the butt of my jokes, as it were, but not in the way the Yuk Yuk's crowd was used to.

My set was taped by the instructor, Avi—the man who would, sixteen months later, become my lover. It's on VHS, so I can no longer watch my youthful bravado, but I used to enjoy hearing his laugh, and the guffaws of my friends in the audience. I don't remember much of my set, but I'm pretty sure there were references to morning sickness and placentas, as well as lactation party tricks. I wouldn't be surprised if the regulars in the audience asked for their money back.

I recently found this list of subject headings from emails I sent to my daughters over the years, which Emma curated and saved because apparently she and her sister found them entertaining:

This is your mother speaking

Your mama

Your mama is a cool lesbian!

My friend from round robin art group is setting me up with this woman

The gays xmas eve

Xmas food, part deux

Lox hold-up

What are your iphone measurements?

I'm going in an airplane!

Look at me on Wifi in Barcelona!

Ok, for real, really, now, really?

Hat!

Racism sucks

Amazon/Giant White Girl

Woof

Falling over tree

What I learned about sex toys

Eyes, teeth, uterus, other body parts

Girly bits surgery

Grrr

I quit muffs!

Tattoo font

Grandbabies

Top secret elf info

Am I with it, or what?

No, I was wrong

Fun, wow

Let's do this at union station!

Butlers

Cat, bag

Smokin' hot or fizzled out?

Smoking hot boy

Let the drooling begin

Is anybody awake over there?

Exhaustipooped?

I'm in a happy parallel universe

Yay, me

I'm very famous this month

Famous for my donuts

More evidence your mother is fabulous

This has been a message from your
mother

Château en Espagne

I HAVE ALWAYS loved road trips. With my parents, I only ever vacationed in Ontario, and not very often, given my dad's discomfort with new surroundings. My mum and I met up with my aunt and cousin several times at The Opinicon, a charming hundred-year-old lodge on the Rideau Canal, where the furnishings, menu, and waitresses never changed. The two of us went to the Caribbean once, with my mum's oldest friend and her teenage daughter, which was an extravagance. They let us drink piña coladas underage in the bar and dance with extraordinarily handsome local men, whom I now realize were there for the enjoyment of the single ladies. I naïvely went off with one of these men to see a "special beach" while the mothers were napping one afternoon. I was lucky—he graciously took no for an answer and walked me back to the resort. My only misadventure that trip was a severe sunburn from a paddleboat ride. But in general, we stuck close to home.

I used to take my daughters to that same Ottawa Valley lodge, where resistance to modernization kept prices low, and the comfort food never disappointed. The place looked like a Wes Anderson movie set. The best part was always the drive. There is nothing like being trapped in a car for a few hours together to facilitate meaningful conversation, punctuated by thunderous singing and bursts of gut-busting laughter. The girls always liked to make me laugh to the point that I had to reach for my asthma inhaler. Car rides with them are among my happiest parenting memories.

I took them to see family in England when they were thirteen and seven, and we had the same kind of quality time on trains, playing rummy and eating Cadbury Flake bars. Sophie was a fantastic traveller, even at that age, curious about everything, chatty with everybody, and never whiny about all the walking. I wanted the girls to meet my mum's cousin, who was like a favourite aunt to me; she also got cancer young, but it was in remission that summer. Sophie really bonded with her husband, who unfortunately stopped sending Christmas cards after I took up with a woman. My relatives' Lancashire accents were so strong, it took a couple of days for the girls to make out a word they said, but before long we were all laughing our fool heads off. I remember us belting out Abba songs during a group Ferris wheel ride in Blackpool.

When Emma was nineteen, I re-negotiated my

mortgage in such a way that I could buy a car after some years without wheels, mostly because I wanted to drive the girls east from Toronto to Halifax for the start of Emma's second year at university. We set off in our little Toyota named Marigold. Despite being an overzealous planner, I quite like to drive without a fixed destination. On that trip, I didn't book accommodation except for the first night; I let the road take us through New England until we eventually got to Mahone Bay, Nova Scotia for a few days by the ocean before leaving Emma and meandering back through New Brunswick and Quebec's Eastern Townships. We happily indulged our mutual love of seafood on that trip and sang along with kd lang to Roy Orbison's "Crying" probably fifty times in the car.

Tight finances limited our travels together after that, but the year Emma turned twenty-five, she came into some money due to a mistake in my grandfather's last Will. The heirs should have stopped at my generation, but the wording was such that all his "issue" at the time of his daughters' deaths were entitled to some funds when they reached the age of twenty-five, which accidentally included his great-grandchildren. When my mother died, Sophie wasn't born yet, so she was technically left out, but Emma went halfsies with her. And then, out of the blue, those marvelous women invited me to Spain. There is an expression in French, un *château en Espagne*, that means something luxurious but unattainable, equivalent to "a castle in the air." I had thought my tourist days were over; I never expected to see Gaudi's actual château.

Sophie had been in Europe since that fateful July when I was turfed from the condo I shared with Kate. She'd earned her final high school credit on a study tour of historic cities and stayed to do some WOOFing (working on organic farms). Emma joined her in October—I admit I'd urged her to go be a good influence on her sister—and then we all met up in Barcelona for ten days, their treat. I wasn't sure I'd be able to fly, given a midlife problem with claustrophobia, but a round of cognitive behavioural therapy and a fistful of Ativan did the trick. I hadn't been across the Atlantic since the funeral of my mum's cousin more than a decade earlier and hadn't indulged in this kind of trip filled with art and history since I was eighteen. I was awed by Gaudi, smitten with Miro, and impressed by Picasso, whose misogyny I had not yet figured out.

We drank sangria and some of the laughter of our earlier travels together returned. We cracked up reading menus badly translated into English, featuring "lamb chaps," "shrimps with coats," and "deking eggs." There were bumpy bits, naturally. Emma and I were crashing Sophie's gap year; she'd been quite enjoying her solo sojourn, despite getting a bit carried away in the wild oats department. She needed to go off on her own some of the time. But there were some beautiful moments, and one memorable night in particular.

Because Emma makes connections wherever she goes, she naturally had a Cree friend from British Columbia who had a Peruvian friend living in Barcelona, and introductions were made. He was a gay pastry chef who had moved to Spain to escape the homophobia of his hometown, where his bakery business had suffered because of his rumoured sexual orientation. His liberation had been somewhat hampered when his father arrived to live with him after his mother's death. At that point, he finally came out to his father, whose acceptance was a condition of joining him, and they were making it work.

Miguel was a most gracious tour guide. We went out for tapas with him and his papa, and had a meal of ceviche at their apartment, and then he organized a nocturnal circuit of gay establishments for us. He was very interested to talk to me about the ease of my life as an out lesbian, and glad to have company for some explicitly LGBT tourism. I had not been barhopping in nearly thirty years, and then only a handful of times. Here I was reliving a past I never really had, with my grown kids in tow.

We started at a fancy wine bar that was entirely black and neon pink—a place to see and be seen, and to drink pink champagne. Our next destination was a lesbian pool hall, where we rather stuck out. I was the only lesbian of the bunch but hopeless at both billiards and Spanish. Emma spoke Spanish and could sort of handle a pool cue but describes herself as flamingly heterosexual. Sophie settled in at the bar for tequila shots. Miguel and I strolled around the room, arm in arm, discussing romance in his broken English. After that, we hit up his favourite boy bar, where we were the only women and the only foreigners. Friendly, handsome men kept buying drinks for us exotic Canadians. Around four in the morning, we left Miguel on the dance floor and went for pizza. For that one night, all three of us were nineteen years old, without a care in the world.

Radical Acceptance

I AM CRAWLING ALONG the 401, too tired to be safely driving; it's the morning rush hour and chucking down with rain. Twenty-six-year-old Sophie is in the passenger seat and I am trying to keep her alive. It's day three of this mission.

I had travelled to Guelph, where she lived, on the morning of Mother's Day. I was already burnt out, but she wanted to take me to lunch. First, I had crossed the city to borrow a car, then gotten trapped by street closures for a marathon. It had taken me two hours just to break free of downtown Toronto, by which time I was sobbing and had to pee so badly that I went back to my own west-end apartment.

I don't typically sob on the Gardiner Expressway, but I'd had a week of constant calls and texts from Sophie, as she struggled with a steep mood nosedive, and I was scared shitless. She had just spent nine weeks in hospital in Toronto and was still very vulnerable. She'd checked herself into the psych ward in Guelph for one night but checked herself out again. It was very uncomfortable for her to go to her local hospital because, by this time, she was most of the way through her social work degree and already working and volunteering in the field. In a small community, this guaranteed running into colleagues, professors, and clients at the mental health facility that served the whole region.

She had been doing her best to keep herself safe, but when I finally arrived, it was clear we had to get to a hospital somewhere. Her partner was at work. When he got home, we all agreed we'd hold off until the morning, when Sophie had an appointment scheduled with her psychiatrist. We'd ask his advice about where to go. I shared the bed with Sophie, her boyfriend took the couch. Sleepless night number one.

The doctor didn't really have any good ideas, apart from going back to the Toronto hospital she had entered in winter and not exited until spring. She had been desperately, diligently researching options, and wanted to try another southern Ontario hospital that offered a mood disorder program. She'd asked to be referred there but couldn't get in that way. She was told an alternative route might be through its emergency department. Off we went.

The triage system was that of a butcher shop: take a number from a red dispenser on the wall and wait to be served. After three hours, a woman who could not touch-type spent fifteen minutes entering the names of all the medications Sophie was on. After four more hours, we were told there were no beds, and in any case the mood program was only available to outpatients. But Sophie could sleep on the floor if she wanted. On the fucking floor.

It was dark by this time. We decided we would have to try for a bed back in Toronto again, but I couldn't tackle the trip at that hour without risking both our lives, so I drove us all back to Sophie's apartment. Sleepless night number two. By this time, I was pretty much crying all the time, in a most un-rock-like departure from my normally steady calm. Not only was I completely fried, but I had missed two doses of my own antidepressant, which is a time-sensitive one. The next morning marked day three in the same clothes. Though I had showered, I'd pragmatically ditched my less-than-fresh undies. Before we hit the highway, I stopped in the downpour for coffee and gas, and got soaked to the skin. Of the two of us, any observer would have pegged me as the one needing medical assistance.

We waited in a room full of people in various states of distress, but this was CAMH (Centre for Addiction and Mental Health, at the former Clarke Institute site), where the staff were highly skilled, consistently respectful, and very kind. I went to the washroom and discovered that I had managed to rip a huge hole in the crotch of my linen pants, which I was wearing commando. The only saving grace was that I had a short dress over top. My daughter Emma mocks this fashion choice of mine, along with my bold colour palette (she says my style combines the aesthetic of Miss Frizzle from *The Magic School Bus* and the paintings of Piet Mondrian), but it served me well on this occasion.

When I got back to the waiting room, a woman who had been silently detoxing on a gurney suddenly raised her head and declared, "The LED lights are sucking out all my sparkles!" I turned to Sophie, explained about my wardrobe malfunction, and said, "Mine are falling out directly onto the floor." That made her laugh.

In fairly short order, Sophie was back on the ward she'd vacated the previous month. In fact, she was back in the same room, in the same bed, down but not out, her resilience something to behold. Once she'd been admitted, a friend picked me up. We stopped for malted milkshakes and I told her the commando/sparkles story; we laughed until I cried a bunch more. I got home, downed my medication, ditched some reeking perch that had expired in my fridge, and went to bed.

The next night, I was supposed to read at an event. I had won an emerging writer's prize for a story about my suburban upbringing. I could not go. I did not have the wherewithal to read about my father's mental illness while my daughter was in hospital. The organizer could not have been more understanding despite my last-minute cancellation; her own daughter had mental health issues, and she told me she'd spent years never knowing if she could commit to attending anything. That also made me cry a lot, but then I slept for twelve hours.

The following day was my fifty-fifth birthday, but I resisted the urge to reflect on either the past or coming year. I joked with Sophie that all it signified was eligibility for Shoppers Drug Mart's seniors' discount on Thursdays. I went to work. In the evening, I went to my support group for people with mentally ill loved ones. We discussed the concept of *radical acceptance* developed by Marsha Linehan as part of dialectical behaviour therapy, which is enjoying a heyday in psych circles. The simple idea, reflecting most if not all religions and philosophies but seldom practiced successfully, is to acknowledge that while we can change many things, there are some problems we can't solve. Reality is very stubborn. We can't win a fight with the past. We might as well accept the unacceptable, especially if it's already happened, because to do anything else sucks worse.

Emma had sent me a Mother's Day card that proclaimed in bold type, "You are a radical woman." I could only hope it was true.

Ms. Manners
(or The Perils of Online Dating)

THE FIRST TIME I sought out women for purposes of dating, it involved actual letters, handwritten on paper. People placed ads in the back of Toronto's *NOW* magazine (earnest ones, not the kind that require the pixilation of nipples and anuses), and I answered one. A smattering of dates resulted, but the letter-writing proved the most enjoyable part of the whole endeavour.

There was a self-imposed dry spell, while I supported my children through the loss of their father, before I felt I had a spare ounce of energy or emotion to offer anyone else. One day when she was a young teen, Sophie ventured the opinion that it might do me good to get laid. The cheek! It's possible I had built up some discernible tension.

Off into the wild lavender yonder I went. I had one date with a woman who told me she specialized in bedding both halves of a straight couple, either together or separately. It was a pastime with an extra element of challenge, I suppose, like the *Globe and Mail* holiday crossword. I decided I'd prefer the crossword.

I took myself downtown to a venue in the gay village for a women's dance one night, in Pride season, to meet up with a jazz singer. Just that one detail was intriguing enough to get me out of the house. We located each other on a patio, and she told me she just needed to take her vitamins before we went inside. I wasn't sure why she needed to announce this, until she hauled out a giant tote bag and set a good dozen bottles of assorted natural supplements on the table. It turned out she was big into alternative medicine, which is fine with me, but spending fifteen minutes swallowing tablets and tinctures seems like a decidedly tenth date kind of thing. She did not, it became apparent, believe in deodorant, natural or chemical. And she told me with some satisfaction that she owned Crocs in every colour. I feigned an early morning.

At a coffee shop, I met a woman who had indicated she'd recently left her husband but had been in previous same-sex relationships. I was curious to note she was still wearing a wedding band and a very blingy diamond engagement ring. She and her husband were still under the same roof, and she told me he spent his evenings sobbing outside her bedroom door. I beat a hasty retreat.

I had dinner with a one-armed electrician, who had chosen her career field after losing her arm in an electrocution accident. I thought that took chutzpah and was fascinated that she had started learning Hindi because she was so moved by the films of Deepa Mehta. She ordered for both of us, which was off-putting, but it was an Indian restaurant and she requested (and paid for) pretty much everything on the menu, so I chose to be gracious about it. I was interested enough to invite her over for a game night at my house, where she initiated a shouting match with another guest who merely expressed a difference of opinion. Lesson learned: always introduce a prospective suitor into a group situation very early on.

At that time, in the mid-2000s, online dating etiquette demanded that if someone sent you a message, you replied with either an inviting "tell me more" or a polite "no thank you." Ten years later, when I waded back in, such was not the case.

After the disillusionment of my first longish lesbian relationship, I concluded that my picker was broken, and until I could somehow repair it, I should not attempt to pick prospective romantic partners. I vowed to live alone—for the first time in my whole life—and to take proper time to recover from a truly horrid breakup. But that is not what I did. I had barely weaned off my daily forty-minute crying jag when a friend asked if she could introduce me to a woman who'd been divorced for about a year (from another woman) and lived conveniently close by. Against my better judgement, I agreed. As always, the fear of loneliness was insinuating its way into my decision-making process.

Brenda was lovely, and attractive, and extremely attentive. I didn't feel a deep connection, but I didn't want one. I told her as plainly as I could that I was rebounding and had to take things at a crawl. Within a month, she had told me she loved me and started planning our summer holidays. I felt terrible when I broke her heart a little, because I know how easy it is to ignore evidence to the contrary and cling to the hope that dating will turn into more.

I really did keep to myself for a good long while. Every now and again I would peek at the popular lesbian dating sites, where some of the same characters from a decade before were still looking for love. I would log off without uploading a profile. Fortunately for me, menopause had dragged my libido down to a normal range, from its previous setting of "nineteen-year-old boy."

My fairy godson gave me a demonstration of Tinder one spring day while we were sipping Americanos in High Park and told me everyone of every age was on it, and not just for hookups. (This chosen family member is my daughter's best friend. I introduced him to a ridiculously handsome fellow with whom he had a romance, thus earning me the title of fairy godmother.) I took a peek and quickly shut off my computer in abject fear of the judgy swiping. But the exercise motivated me to try a paid online dating site, where I assumed I would find a more mature clientele.

It was better. There were about a hundred women in my vicinity and age range. After culling those who couldn't use punctuation, those passionate about sports, and those who posted pictures of their pets in lieu of themselves, my prospects shrunk to about a dozen. I sent out a few feelers, determined to get my money's worth.

One was directed to a woman whose photo I recognized straight away. She was a well-known author; I'd read all her books, including a memoir, so I knew we had some experiences in common. I thought it would be odd to use her pseudonym and pretend I didn't know who she was, so I addressed her by her real name and referred to her writing. She took down her profile immediately. I feel badly that a deserving Canadian author may have missed out on some action because of me.

Clearly, protocol demands that one not "out" someone from their photo. I had also sent a very short, casual message to a woman I had met a few times, using her real name and mine, and she did not reply. Now it's going to be awkward when I bump into her. It would be much less awkward if she'd simply written, "Oh hello. Can't say I'm interested, but good luck on this site," or words to that effect. I always made a point of saying, "thanks but no thanks" to women who had the gumption to contact me. To ignore a greeting, online as in person, seems needlessly callous. These people haven't affronted or insulted you. You're all on the damn Internet for the sole purpose of connecting. The routine rudeness flummoxes me.

I had one encounter that was a primer in poor manners. A woman contacted me and suggested we talk on the phone, which she felt was a suitable commitment of time halfway between chatting online and hauling ourselves to a café. I don't really enjoy talking on the phone, but I agreed. Her first questions were, "Is that your real picture?" and "Is that your real age?" I thought perhaps she had reason to be skeptical, and let it slide. Then she wanted to know which newspaper I read. I told her. She said, "Well, that article on Wednesday about the link between Council and the transit lobbyists was based on information I uncovered and made public." I had to confess I had not seen the article in question. She snarked, "I thought you said you read the *Star*."

It got worse. She told me her real name, so while she prattled on about all the many causes she supported and injustices she fought, I Googled her. There she was, looking drop-dead gorgeous, holding up signs at various and sundry protests, sometimes in a very small ragtag group, admonishing everything from the treatment of chickens to the plight of refugees. When a bit more clicking linked her to the anti-vaccine movement, I was done. I started playing online Scrabble while she kept talking. She finally wrapped up with, "Unless you're a full-time activist, I don't think it makes sense for us to get together." I wished her luck in her quest for such a person.

Honestly, I would rather never have sex again until the day I die than be forced to go on even one more first date. Apparently, a lot of people feel the same way. Recent statistics reveal that a good thirty per cent of Canadian households contain one lone person. For a lot of us, the cure for solitude isn't to pair off. Many of the old ideas about coupledom are in disrepute, and family is being redefined, which is all to the good. That's what feminism is for, among other things.

I have lamented the tiny size of my tribe though. At various times in the past, I've tried to semi-formally add members to my family, especially when my daughters were young and so bereft of blood relatives. Dan's family was almost entirely absent. His partner stayed connected, which she was under no obligation to do, but then again obligation is a poor motive for maintaining relationships. I recruited an "uncle" and "goddess-mother" but they wandered off after a while, furthering my girls' sense of abandonment. As adults, they collected their own mentors to fill some of those voids. My chosen family at this point includes a fine assortment of folks. I've shared my home with foster youth, international students, and roommates, because research clearly shows it's healthier to dine with a companion.

My Year of Simple Pleasures

AS I APPROACHED my forty-ninth birthday, some years ago now, I felt the impending arrival of fifty keenly... but not with trepidation. More with the anticipation of a milestone worth celebrating in a creative way. I've never experienced any formal rituals to mark important transitions, mostly because I was raised in a secular family in a Western environment. I had no confirmation, Bat Mitzvah, or other coming-of-age ceremony. I'm certainly not part of a culture that celebrates a woman's transition from her fertile years to her crone years. Not everyone likes the word "crone," but I do. Within the triad maiden-mother-crone, it's certainly the stage least fraught with worry, and characterized by wisdom and good judgement. Just because we can't remember why we went in the kitchen doesn't mean we don't have invaluable insights to share.

I decided that an enjoyable way to count down to fifty would be to set out to complete fifty activities in the year leading up to my birthday. It was a handy way to trick myself into having fun—give me a list, and I will dutifully tick off every item. My list had to be manageable in terms of cost and time, because I was busy running a retail arts business that required my presence at least six days out of seven. I solicited suggestions from friends, and soon had an inspiring long-list to whittle down to the final selection. I eliminated anything that smacked of self-improvement or served too functional a purpose (no mastering of PowerPoint or cleaning out of drawers) and kept most of the activities within Toronto city limits. Some involved revisiting moments from the distant past, others took me out of my comfort zone. Here is a small sample.

1. Fudging It

My mother was famous for her peanut butter raisin fudge. Andy was not a stereotypical suburban cookie-baking wife and mother. But she did her best to fit in by doing things like making fudge for the school bake sale. I remember these fudge episodes for two reasons...my mother would stand at the stove cursing under her breath for a really long time, and Mr. Poole, the head custodian at my primary school, would buy up the whole batch at every fundraiser; nobody else got to taste even a morsel. It really was good fudge.

I have moved my mother's recipe box from place to place for thirty years. It must once have been orderly, because there are index cards scattered throughout that say "appetizers" or "dessert" on them. But when I came into its possession, it looked like it had been through a gorse bush backwards. I didn't venture in until I decided to try to replicate that fabled fudge. Alas, I could not find the recipe anywhere among the hundreds of bits of paper. I had to go online, where I found recipes calling for marshmallow fluff (clearly a cheater's shortcut), recipes requiring a lot of patient stirring to get the concoction to the "soft ball" stage (my mother's method), and another which required some boiling but did not seem unreasonably onerous. So I used that one. To me, the resulting taste was pretty much as I remember. Heat applied to vast quantities of sugar and peanut butter is all but guaranteed to satisfy.

While rifling through the recipe box, I found a few in my grandmother's handwriting (though I don't think I'll make her classic tooth-chipping treacle toffee). Some were on dog-eared cards "from the kitchen of" friends and relatives, and I could instantly taste them off the page: the meatballs, the crab dip, the "mousse" inflated with Dream Whip. The box as a whole offers a trip through Ontario middle-class suburban culture from the sixties through the eighties as expressed through its cuisine. There's some revolting stuff in there, much of it involving aspic, creamed soups, and canned fruit. Apparently jellied salads are back in vogue among hipsters, though I can't imagine why. I'll never make most of this crap, but I can't throw anything out. The recipes cut from newspapers and magazines are too interesting as archival documents. I often seek out such ephemera from my childhood to help me make sense of the life my parents and I led in that preherstoric era on the planet Etobicoke.

I often wonder if I've "turned into my mother," as the saying goes. I don't feel I had enough time with her to make this assessment. I'm approaching the age she was when she died, but our life experiences had diverged dramatically by middle age. I wish there was someone around to say, "Your mum used to make that face when she was amused," or "Your mum always said that when she was frustrated." But there is no one. All I can do is look at her hands on the ends of my arms, and her feet on the ends of my legs, and wonder about our similarities.

As I age, it's increasingly Lloyd Stanley Breen who stares back at me in the mirror. Seeing his face makes me miss him too.

My favourite recipes—like most of the paper that has trailed through my life—are categorized and neatly held in a binder. My mother was also very organized (perhaps the recipe box fell victim to the cancer that so confused her thoughts in her final months). But I harbour some of the same secret messy places she had. My towels and sheets, for example, are always put away in the linen closet, but in an anarchic scrambled bundle. Nothing can compel me to fold a fitted sheet. My gift wrapping, ribbons, and tags form a similarly wild nest, but are contained within a bin always in its place in the cupboard. It's a source of sensory pleasure to dig through all that colour and texture while hunting for a sheet of tissue paper. My underwear drawer is a jumble of panties, bras I never wear, and socks, some bundled into pairs, many widowed. I like being weird in ways my mum was weird, and I find a kind of joy in my own inconsistency.

2. Hey, What's SUP?

This fifty-list experience touched on two recurring themes of mine: 1. I love Toronto, and 2. Aging is kind of great. My adventurous friend Didi and I tried stand-up paddleboarding (SUP, to those in the know) on Lake Ontario. We were both surprised to find the waterfront bustling with paddleboards, kayaks, canoes, and dragon boats. All kinds of people—the whole glorious diversity of this city—were enjoying the lake in ways we hadn't in a generation. We saw a good array of bird life as well—swans, loons, geese, ducks, egrets, and cormorants. Our instructor was one of a pair of lovely young sisters who offer paddleboarding as well as yoga on paddleboards. The latter might have to wait for a later date. It was enough to stay on the blasted thing without also assuming downward dog.

Once we got our sea legs, it was pretty straightforward—keeping in mind that we were in utterly calm water inside the harbour wall. Didi and I each fell in twice for good measure, and the lake and air were the perfect temperature to make these little dips refreshing. Neither of us gave a hoot what we looked like. So what if our legs were trembling like newborn Bambi for the first ten minutes? So what if our wet clothes clung to our fleshy bits? I've got nobody to impress. I unselfconsciously paddled sitting down for a while, to let my feet rest. Because I finally have self-esteem.

When I was in middle school, I had the particular misfortune to be taught gym (girls only, as was the norm) by a woman—let's call her Mrs. Spitz—who seemed bound and determined to destroy any shred of self-esteem we might be thinking of carrying with us into puberty. Her comments made us feel dirty and unpleasant in every way. She told us we stank (literally) and that our greasy hair and acne were revolting.

It wasn't the era of "everyone wins!" but rather of clear winners (sporty, pretty) and losers (ungainly, different). When I found one track event I was pretty good at—high jump—Mrs. Spitz actively tried to dissuade me from competing in a city meet for which I had qualified, on the grounds that my good performance was a fluke. She said, "I think we all know who deserves to go," referring to the girl who cleared the next-best height after me. Even though I had practiced and practiced to earn my spot, she thought I should cede it to the other competitor, who was an excellent athlete. But the girl in question had qualified in virtually every other event and had plenty to keep her busy at the meet, so she was only too happy to leave the high jumping to others. As it happened, I did my best jump ever at the city meet, which Mrs. Spitz did not acknowledge. Then I shared a doobie in the washroom with a girl from my music class.

This unhappy creature was also assigned to teach us "health," and I still remember her answer to one girl's question: "Can we swim with our periods?" She said, "Yes and no," and when asked to elaborate, repeated, "Just what I said, yes and no." Now, I can see that she was a woman terrified of her own body and caught up in society's ambivalence about the growing influence of second-wave feminism, but it really was a shame she was in a position to pass her extreme discomfort on to us. I spent my teen years nervous about all of my orifices and unpredictable limbs, dubious about teams of any kind, and generally contemptuous of sports. No wonder it took me so long to get up on that paddleboard.

3. Dinner for One

My to-do list was decidedly not about self-improvement, but that didn't preclude learning a few new tricks, especially in the kitchen, where I was a huge disappointment to myself. I have never had the patience for domestic labour. I did not grow up doing any because I was a privileged kid whose house was cleaned weekly by a paid contract worker, and our food mostly came out of convenient boxes and tins. I watched Emma make browned-butter carrots for the holidays one time, and it seemed she stood for hours at the stove, whisking until the butter was just right. I said I wouldn't bother with that step, to which she replied, "Well, then they wouldn't be browned-butter carrots, Mum. They'd just be carrots." Point taken.

After I left my husband, who had done all the cooking exceedingly well, I was hard-pressed to feed my children any variety of foodstuffs, especially when each of them experimented with vegetarianism but not at the same time. When a parent at the school offered a cooking lesson in a silent auction, I placed the winning bid. I'm sure she expected to be teaching a teenage boy about to leave for university, but she got me. She showed me how to make veggie lasagna, and the result was mouth-watering. My children claimed that I served this dish every single time we had dinner guests for the next ten years. Which is not wrong.

For the first couple of months of solitary living, it was kind of fun to eat anything I wanted, directly out of the container or straight from the pot. But dining like a bachelor definitely lost its charm, and curiously, did not prove optimal for my health. I went to the Bay and acquired some proper knives and a few different pans with the help of a salesperson who assumed I was kitting out my child's first apartment. I conquered chili, which was more exciting than it might sound given my culinary impairment, and one day decided to tackle Thai red curry from scratch. I would normally have waited until I could invite guests to dine with me, but I had a pocket of time at home (rare), and a fridge full of food (very rare), so I decided to seize the moment and cook for myself. I enjoyed the fruits of my labour watching *Jeopardy*, which is my idea of an excellent date with myself. I experienced the same satisfaction I get from using household items I've made myself (like my potholders and dish cloths, shampoos and deodorants), and even though my kitchen was traditionally a place reserved for baking (which I love), I began to hang out there more often.

My stubbornness adds, I'll readily admit, a further obstacle to my gastronomic success. I rarely follow recipes because I have a general distaste for doing what I'm told. I question authority, even when it's coming from the GPS lady in the car. Everyone seems to use Google Maps when going places, but I'm a renegade. For decades, I managed fine with beat-up roadmaps and posted signs. Sometimes I took a scenic route, it's true, but I never cared, and I never got seriously lost. Sometimes my dishes take the scenic route.

For all my love of handmaking, I behave in much the same manner when engaged in most crafty undertakings—too many fiddly steps, and I start improvising. I am what my friends generously refer to as an "artistic" knitter, meaning I deviate from the pattern to the point of sometimes ending up with a different garment altogether. On holiday once, Emma and Sophie watched me crochet an item that turned out to be a serviceable and pretty cute sunhat, but for several hours there, it was unclear what it might turn out to be. I've had scarves turn into table runners and table runners into doormats, but there's no harm in that; in fact, the element of surprise is an added bonus. I rarely care what I make—I just need to have yarn in my hands whenever I am sitting down. I tell myself I am doing something useful besides watching TV, but really I am self-soothing.

My brain is decidedly lopsided. For all my administrative talent and list-making, I cannot put together Ikea furniture to save my life. (I do like saying the product names and making up pretend ones, however. *Fackförening*, anyone? Actually, that means *trade union*, but it's a great word that sounds like a place to store garden tools.) In fact, to try to assemble furniture makes me homicidal, and I have been urged by witnesses never to attempt it again. I know better than to approach any task that involves fitting things together, not even a picture puzzle. I loathe them. I am not the sort of lesbian who can install shelves or pack the trunk for camping, and I'm okay with that. There are plenty of lesbians who can't take a ball of yarn and accidentally end up with a hat, but as a demographic whole, I'd say we serve all the needs of the community.

I also know I will never be Martha Stewart. Comedian Mary Walsh once brilliantly satirized the decor mogul in a sketch where she hot-glued 400 individual cranberries onto a wreath; at the end of it, she drunkenly laments, "I will never get that time back!" That's how I feel about most domestic tasks, though I am trying to slow down and build my patience incrementally. I have taught myself to make focaccia bread, which has to rise for an hour. It's a start.

4. Burgers and Bowling in the 'Burbs

Bowling made the agenda, and since the Etobicoke Bowlerama (now demolished) was the most convenient alley I could find, I thought I'd add a second impromptu activity: to dine at the nearby burger joint of my youth.

The unfortunately named Apache Burgers has been around longer than I have. A Google search to locate directions for my companions brought up a list of 365 things to do in Etobicoke, and visiting this place ranked number one. There is no way to collect accurate data, but I'm pretty sure that one hundred per cent of Etobicoke teenagers north of Brown's Line and south of Albion had dates here in the seventies, and perhaps continue to do so to this day. My first date with my first boyfriend took place here, after a movie at the (also demolished) Humber Cinema.

It was 1979 and I was fifteen, dating a nineteen-year-old boy. I had met him when I was thirteen and volunteering at my grandmother's nursing home to make my dad happy. Dave had a summer job there as a cleaner. Apparently, he had the hots for me then, but a seventeen-year-old dating a thirteen-year-old seems even ickier than a nineteen-year-old dating a fifteen-year-old, so he didn't ask me out. Two years later, I saw him on the Anglesey bus, and he asked for my number. The four-year age gap was still a bit embarrassing (for him—for me, it was something to brag about), so he tended to lie about my age. I was his second girlfriend, but we were both virgins. Poor guy must have been itching to get rid of that label. He patiently waited until my sixteenth birthday to consummate our relationship without fear of legal troubles. Once that was done, we were free to fuck like rabbits in the comfort of his bed. In his house full of introverts, it was normal for everyone to retreat to their corners after dinner. The three boys would get up from the table and go to their respective rooms, taking their girlfriends with them. Their mum was no fool—and did everyone's laundry, poor woman—but nothing was said about the rampant sexual activity going on under that west Etobicoke roof most nights of the week. I remember wondering how adults, who were at liberty to have sex anytime they liked, managed to get anything else done.

Dave had finished high school after Grade 12, which at that time meant he did not qualify for university admission. He worked full-time at an unskilled job and was under no pressure to leave the nest. He had disposable income, so he liked to take me out in his Volkswagen Rabbit. On our second date, the day after our first, we went roller skating at the old Terrace rink on Mutual Street (now demolished, of course). Sometimes we went to sleazy airport strip hotels to hear his friends' terrible cover bands. He was a pretty good guitar player and, like a great many suburban teenagers, imagined a musical career might be just around the corner.

I have wondered why I picked someone with whom I had little in common for my first real foray into romance (not counting miscellaneous groping sessions and a few

short bouts of "going around" with boys), and I've concluded that he was a safe choice. He was perfectly sweet
and overly attentive. Eventually, he went to trade college to
learn about some newfangled gadget called the computer,
and probably ended up in a secure, reasonably interesting
job from which he will soon retire comfortably.

This is the story I told my daughter, her beau, my
fairy godson, and his beau, over burgers. I showed them
a picture of my BF and me, and Emma graciously suggested that two 1979 dweebs equal two 2013 hipsters,
though I'm quite sure her math is wrong. Nobody could
quite get past Dave's luscious pornstache.

Stuffed to the gills with burgers (and in my case, a
malted milkshake), my party of five headed over to the
Bowlerama to test the hypothesis that I can bowl worth
shit. Keep in mind, I was the kid who always got picked
last for teams at school. I cannot throw or catch. I have
been known to blame my eyesight and Mrs. Spitz from
middle school, but it is a general ineptitude that is responsible for my lifelong failure at any sport involving hurling
an object through space. Nobody would suspect me of
being a good bowler, least of all me.

Imagine my surprise when, a couple of years before, I
had found myself filling in on an all-lesbian bowling team
at a fundraiser for the Toronto Rape Crisis Centre, and I
was *good!* I came second only to our team captain, a fine
bowler from way back. I helped our team get the highest
score of all the other teams at the event. My then-partner
was stunned. She questioned whether aliens had borrowed

me for some experiments and left a replacement identical in every way except for hand-eye coordination. Ever since that night, I'd wanted to bowl again to see if it was beginner's luck, or if I actually had a modicum of skill.

This time around, I did not display the same prowess, nor did I suck. My score was pretty much in the middle. Emma won the first game, causing us to conclude I had transferred my bowling genes on to her. Her boyfriend won the second game, even though his wild pre- and post-throw gyrations had me convinced he was going to go hurtling into somebody else's lane. My fairy godson showed fine balletic form in his approach, but more power than precision. His boyfriend did not experience immediate success and switched briefly to the granny method of rolling the ball between his legs, which was quite eye-catching given his 6'7" frame. He later found his groove and managed a strike. We drank mediocre Canadian beer, glowed in the black light, sang along to the pounding music, and had a genuinely good old Etobicoke time.

My year of simple pleasures was both grounding and uplifting. It included tap dancing, bird watching, wine tasting, and guerilla gardening. I went to an opera, an observatory, and a bingo game. I made jam, scones, and even a rug out of old political T-shirts. There were a lot of suggestions that I couldn't get to, but maybe one day before I turn sixty, I will turn around in a crowded elevator and calmly announce, "I suppose you're wondering why I gathered you all here today...."

Unlearning

EMMA SEES THE WORLD as it is, perhaps more clearly than any of us. Others sometimes see Emma as the one who came through unscathed, the one who triumphed over adversity—and that's bullshit. Trying to keep your family members alive is right up there with trying to stay alive, trauma-wise.

Emma was ten when I left her dad; up until that point, she'd had a decade of unbridled fun with him, but not just that. They had a close and mostly healthy relationship. They shared ideas and laughs; their connection was deep and genuine. Dan managed pretty well until Emma was an adolescent; his destructive behaviour dramatically increased in frequency and scope just as she was starting the transition to adulthood. Emma was the person Dan called after his final DUI—the one where his license was suspended. After his car accident, he'd spent the day drinking at his favourite bar in Parkdale, where she found him somewhat battered but mostly unharmed. His shirt was ripped at the shoulder. She guided him home. She had just turned sixteen.

Like me, and like my own father as a teen, her response was to achieve, to accomplish, to excel. She has hunkered down, committing herself to research and activism as an academic working in alliance with Indigenous peoples. I learn something new every time I talk to her.

We all like to think our generation will be the one to set old family patterns ablaze, to toss the whole damned drafting table onto the bonfire and dance around the ashes completely cleansed. But we instinctively gravitate toward the familiar, for better or worse. New research into intergenerational trauma, and the Indigenous understanding that our decisions affect the next seven generations, can at least shed light onto what's going on in the present. We can't eliminate the pain we are bequeathed; we can only deal with it better as time passes.

Emma grappled with the question of whether to have kids who might inherit the family illnesses and/or residual trauma. To my unbridled joy, she went for it and I have a thriving, jolly granddaughter. When I made the decision to have Emma, I gave no thought to what I might be passing on to my children. I was full of the youthful arrogance that allows you to think you occupy your own fabulous island, lush with original, inspired ideas about how to live. This attitude is what keeps humans procreating, I suppose.

I'm well aware that my defence mechanism is to produce my own analgesic, like a cone snail. Temporary numbness is sometimes the only way I can keep doing what has to be done. I stop feeling, stop thinking, take naps, and go through the motions, ticking things off my list. I remember when Sophie was hospitalized as a kid, I still baked a fucking chocolate chiffon cake for her school fundraiser. To support the school where she'd been bullied and wouldn't even be returning. Every now and again I have gone all fierce mama bear, particularly in school and hospital settings. Neither extreme is ideal. My very Anglo ancestry favours decorum and a certain amount of denial. I wish I'd had the courage to demand more help for Dan, even if it didn't work. I wish I'd gotten my kids the hell away from him sooner and let him cry foul. I will no doubt continue to be jolted by epiphanies that would have been way more useful decades ago.

I marvel at the expansion of Emma's circle to include a whole raft of different people, including a posse of women she's known since daycare, friends she's made all over Canada and beyond, and Indigenous activists who have provided her with a plethora of perspectives and much-needed kinship. The late Arthur Manuel, a respected Secwépemc leader, was a mentor to Emma, and became a father figure. He was uncompromising, warm, and funny. He taught her to drive in the snow, he teased her, and he challenged her during long conversations over dim sum. He believed in her. His best ever text to her read, "I wish you a wonderful experience decolonizing yourself." Amen to that.

Letting Go, Part I

I DON'T MEAN to trivialize the serious harm caused by body dysmorphia, but I feel I may have a flipped version of the disorder, in which I see not a wrinkly, plump, post-menopausal woman in the mirror, but rather someone fortyish, of average build. I have, however, conceded that my breasts no longer point straight ahead, but instead indicate a spot on the floor a couple of metres in front of me, where I have perhaps dropped something important. I have also discovered what eyelashes are for: mine are the only thing keeping my eyelids from sliding right down and obstructing my view. All my parts are in working order, so it's easy to forget that I could only be described as "middle-aged" if I'm going to live well beyond the birthday that warrants congratulations from the Queen.

When I was young, I don't remember thinking about my body's appearance that much—certainly only a fraction as much as people seem to do now. It was frowned upon to be fat, and of course it was exciting to grow breasts, but I don't remember learning that everything about being a girl is vaguely disgusting and needs either camouflage or improvement, at least not until I encountered Mrs. Spitz in middle school. Maybe I just wasn't paying attention, because I was slim and fair—both valued commodities. My self-worth issues were unrelated to my body image.

My mother may have been pretty with-it and open-minded, but she was also a product of her time. Once, when I was catcalled in her presence as a very young teen, she gave me a jocular backhanded compliment: "Well, you're not hideous, you know!" It wouldn't have occurred to her that a dude in his thirties had no business doing that to a girl. She also seemed to think that "blue balls" was a thing, and worthy of sympathy, back when I was first dating and she was sharing a few anatomical tidbits of information with me. She didn't want me to cause my boyfriend pain, but she wasn't advocating that I put out whenever asked either, so I'm not sure what the takeaway of that discussion was meant to be. A few weeks after my first child's birth, which had involved forceps and an episiotomy you could pass a toaster through, she quietly asked if I was able to have sex again out of concern for my husband's well-being. That one warranted the stink eye, which I was not in the habit of directing her way.

My mother and I tended to see eye to eye on all the important things, and we were a tight duo. It was effortless, at least from my end. I could—and did—phone her every night when I was in university, to get a pep talk about managing my course load. She was the opposite of a helicopter parent, but I bounced everything off her voluntarily. She was my only person, and she was generous and gracious about it, without ever giving unsolicited advice. I felt no compunction about burdening her with my endless stream of minor worries, right up until she got cancer.

Sex was not something we discussed in gory detail. She knew when I was having it and what I was doing for birth control, which I now realize is an unusual level of disclosure right there. It seemed natural for me to share the milestone of my first time with her, and my subsequent adventures. I was only on partner number four when she died, so there wasn't much to tell, but she knew about my every crush and heartache. I even told her about my indiscretion in Louisiana. We never talked about orgasms, whereas my daughters were quite unselfconscious about discussing theirs with me. I remember my daughter Sophie cheerfully bringing up the topic of female ejaculation at breakfast one morning. She asked, "Which hole does the stuff come out of?" I helpfully spurted coffee from my nose.

My mother had told me about her very limited sexual experience when I was a young woman. She wasn't as distressed about this deficiency in her life as I was on her behalf, but she'd come of age in the forties, when women's pleasure was not a priority in most circles. I doubt she had much of a sexual education from my Victorian grandparents. I remember my maternal cousin telling me that her parents were virgins when they married and had never heard of oral sex until some awkward situation arose where she found herself having to explain it to them. They were alarmed. Their sex life involved the missionary position, once a week on Saturdays. My aunt said as much, because we women were all very close. She made it sound like that level of sexual activity was quite pleasant, but plenty. And that was more than my mother got. She wasn't around for my conversion to lesbianism, but would have been very understanding, I think. Her best relationships were all with women, and she was unprejudiced by nature.

One of the things I like best about being a lesbian, besides the swell sex, is being able to present to the world in any one of about a hundred ways. I feel we have more freedom without the constraints of the male gaze, but that might be old-fashioned thinking on my part. Some young straight women are certainly owning their sexuality and fighting rape culture with all their might, against a formidable backlash. The task is daunting, but I feel hopeful that my daughters' generation is equal to it.

I just wish so many naturally beautiful young women wouldn't succumb to the pressure to wax their pubic hair off entirely, or into unnatural shapes, like a topiary of the other sort of bush. It leaves adults looking like prepubescent girls, low on sexy pheromones and liable to catch a chill. It might seem like a minor cause to glom onto, but the popularity of this trend really disturbs me, as a prime example of mass body shaming. I don't think there's been such a successful perpetuation of a beauty myth since the makers of razors realized they were missing out on half the market and launched a merciless campaign to convince women their hairy legs and armpits were repellent. Waxing parlours are as ubiquitous as coffee shops at the moment, but I will not be patronizing any of them.

In lesbian circles, there is the butch/femme divide, of course, but the young folks are tearing those and other labels off, in favour of a much more nuanced and fluid understanding of sexual and gender identities. I'm no longer the only one showing hairy legs under a dress—whatever the genitals between the legs happen to be. I feel no compulsion to shave or wax anywhere (though I will do a little trimming as a courtesy to downstairs guests), unlike my gay brethren, many of whom spend precious time manscaping. I remember a male friend saying as Pride season approached, "It's April—time to stop eating bread." Another lamented, as I stood next to him tucking into hors d'oeuvres at some LGBT event or other, "In my next life, I want to be a lesbian so I can just let myself go." It wasn't meant as an insult, and I didn't take it as one. There's a reason "to let yourself go" means both "to allow yourself to become less attractive" and "to relax completely and enjoy yourself."

Menopause is nothing if not a license to let yourself go. It comes upon half the population with virtually no instructions. There are jokes about hot flashes, dry vaginas, and irritability, but little to help us through these discomforts, and even less to prepare us for the top secret but common phenomenon of sudden-onset phobias, particularly claustrophobia. Perimenopause hit me early, as had puberty. Starting in my mid-forties, I could often be found standing outside my shop in the dead of winter wearing only a T-shirt, perspiration pasting my hair unbecomingly to my head. But the worst manifestation of my chaotically zigzagging hormones was a totally unexpected, brand-new fear of enclosed spaces.

I couldn't ride the subway for a couple of years, and feared I'd never be able to get on a plane again. I would have been convinced I was losing my marbles had several friends my age not been experiencing the exact same thing. My doctor had no idea what I was talking about, but sent me for cognitive behavioural therapy, which helped. My therapist got me singing to myself in elevators; I chose "Climb Every Mountain" from *The Sound of Music*. I consulted a naturopath who pulled out a thick textbook and showed me a passage describing phobias among perimenopausal women. So, it's not entirely classified information, but it sure is underreported.

As I eased my way back onto mass transit, I would pick out a "buddy" to turn to if the subway stopped between stations—my worst nightmare—and sit near that person in case I needed help. A few times I had to say to my unsuspecting support person, "Um, hi, I just want you to know that I might faint if this train doesn't move soon, but it's not a medical emergency, so could you just help me get my head between my knees and not push the emergency alarm?" Even more than being stuck in a tunnel, I feared causing a scene and inconveniencing thousands of commuters. Just reaching out like this prevented me from ever actually fainting on the subway. It's odd behaviour in my culture, asking for assistance from a stranger, but every time I did it, I received utter compassion. People chatted to distract me, and one woman sweetly gave me a mint from her purse. To get from point A to point B in a reasonable amount of time, I had to give up some of my dignity, but I got used to it. Maybe it's the body's way of training us for old age.

There are so many things one *has to* let go of past fifty, but an equal number of things one *gets to* let go of at the half-century mark. It is fantastically liberating to cease giving a fuck as one ages. I've been giving ever fewer fucks since my early forties, but why must it take so long to get to this place? My mother tried to teach me that the verb "should" should be used only sparingly, but I couldn't apply this wisdom for decades.

To acclimatize oneself to letting things go, it's very helpful to recognize the difference between a crisis and an inconvenience; people confuse the two constantly. I remember neighbours who used to be incensed about one thing or another nearly all the time. They were forever knocking at the door, in a snit about our bicycles, our BBQ, our furnace exhaust—none of which had misbehaved or caused offence, particularly. At first, I thought they were homophobic, but really they were just prone to complaining. One day they came to warn of dire consequences if our installation of some new windows caused any glass to fall on the mutual drive, potentially puncturing their $900 tires. I wanted to say, "Cheer up, love, it might never happen!" I also wanted to say, "Unless they allow your car to transform into a hovercraft, who in their right mind buys nine-hundred-dollar tires?" Sadly, the husband from next door died of a massive heart attack in his early sixties; his wife succumbed to illness shortly thereafter. Their early demise might or might not have been related to all the snits, but I feel it's a cautionary tale all the same.

I used to get very wound up about minor injustices, but now that I can see my time is finite, I'm not going to squander any of it on tasks, battles, or relationships that are not integral to my well-being or that of my loved ones. I have lots of fight left in me, but it's targeted toward the things on my anti-bucket list. This is the list I've accumulated of things I want to help undo before I die, such as racial profiling by police, pipeline development on unceded Indigenous land, publicly funded Catholic schools, and Canada's first-past-the-post electoral system.

Flash Mobster

I HAVE ALWAYS WANTED to be part of a flash mob. I love surprises, and I'm big into senseless acts of beauty. For that reason, I've done my fair share of yarn-bombing over the years—attaching coloured swaths of knitting to poles, bike racks, and phone booths (when they existed), simply for the enjoyment of passersby. Anybody's day is going to be better if they've seen a fire hydrant wearing a jaunty hat on their way to the bus stop.

It's hard to sign up for a flash mob, because they are, of necessity, secret. But the opportunity arose prior to a big glittery party to celebrate Buddies in Bad Times' thirty-fifth anniversary during Pride month. Buddies is the world's oldest queer theatre, and I proudly served on its board of directors for two terms. A plot was devised to burst into dance at this event, and word spread that volunteers were needed.

I was in my early fifties, and getting vocal about the continuing usefulness of crones, so I jumped at the chance and made my fortysomething friend join in too. I didn't want it to be nothing but hot young men up there on the stage. Nobody wants to see that. As it turned out, all ages were represented; I wasn't even the oldest dancer. We rehearsed several times, and the piece was choreographed to start out as a duet by the evening's MCs, with more dancers joining two by two from all corners of the room while the audience caught on and got into the spirit. After a few bars, we all ended up onstage to perform some cute moves, then jumped down to involve the crowd in a big finish.

I was dancing my heart out and had enjoyed a couple of drinks generously poured by Buddies' famous bartender, Patricia. I can't fathom how it happened, but when I leapt into the crowd from the stage—a height of perhaps eighteen inches—I dislocated my hip. It hurt like the devil, but I danced it back into place. Having made such a point about the representation of elders in the festivities, there was no way I was going to confess to an injury. I had a few more cocktails, for medicinal purposes, then went home in a cab.

In the morning, I could hardly get out of bed. The pain was excruciating. A friend happened to come by for coffee and sent me post-haste to the emergency room. I was wheeled to the x-ray department to see if my hip was broken. Broken! I didn't know how I would ever live down breaking my hip in a flash mob. I thought I'd have to simply hide from view until it was healed, maybe pretend I was out of the country. It wasn't broken, as it turned out, which the doctor commented was remarkable, given the obvious force with which I had wrenched it from its socket. Hurray for bone density, I guess.

I was sent home with instructions to take tons of anti-inflammatories and keep my leg elevated, but I had shit to do, so I went to my local massage therapist, who is a fantastic healer. I shuffled in like an octogenarian but left the clinic barely limping, like your average weekend warrior who'd hit the trails a bit hard. I wrote one of those Yelp reviews recommending him wholeheartedly for any and all Pride-related flash-mob injuries.

Letting Go, Part II

AMONG THE THINGS I've had to let go of is financial security. I officially fall within the baby boom generation, but like many millennials, I've had only precarious work for much of my life. That's how it is in the not-for-profit sector, where I spent thirty years. My career path was circuitous, with a number of lateral moves, which is also common. When I graduated with a degree in translation in 1986, I thought I could work from home with a small baby. Not so. Freelance translation requires such fast turnaround, it simply could not be fit into nap time. My first post-university job was teaching English to unionized workers at various workplaces in the city, through it was a program run by the labour council. My qualifications for this were good language skills and leftist views. It was part-time and classes were held at shift change, so I could get out a couple of times a week when my husband was home to take over childcare. I remember I made thirty-three dollars an hour—a rate I have never matched since, with the exception of a few consulting gigs.

That job taught me much about my own privilege. My students looked up to me simply because I was born Canadian. I was in awe of them—immigrant women, for the most part, who had sacrificed their comfort and security for the sake of their offspring. Many had also given up social and professional position and respect, taking low-skilled, low-paying jobs here, yet saving to put their kids through university. It seemed absurd that I was their teacher, and as such held in the highest esteem. Teaching English also opened my eyes to the need for adult literacy education; some of my students spoke English as their first language but had only the most rudimentary reading skills, for reasons most often related to poverty, violence, and discrimination.

My education about power and oppression continued when I started working with a literacy advocacy group. I was so engaged in this work, I thought I'd pursue a Master's in adult education, and was accepted to a program at the Ontario Institute for Studies in Education. I didn't get that degree, essentially because there has never been the political will to implement a proper national childcare strategy. My daughter Emma was in an excellent, licensed, not-for-profit daycare from the age of eighteen months. When she began there, our fees were subsidized because my income was low. When I got a better position, I dutifully reported my increased earnings to the ministry in charge and went off subsidy. I went back to that government office when I got into grad school, to reactivate my subsidy. Childcare funding had been frozen in the meantime. No new applicants could be served. Without affordable childcare, I couldn't further my education.

I didn't know how much it would matter down the road. At the time, it was not hard to find work; I got every job I wanted from 1986 to 2000. I spent four years crisscrossing the country working on a marvelous project linking literacy programs to their local museums, with the vision of preserving and telling different kinds of stories than had typically been valued in the past. I got pregnant with Sophie very shortly after taking this job, and since she wouldn't take a bottle, she had to tag along or starve. Cocky feminist that I was, it didn't occur to me that people would object to a workshop facilitator having a baby strapped to her chest...and they didn't. We'd take breaks for me to nurse and participants to smoke, and it all worked out fine. People happily passed the baby around. I remember landing at such a small airport in Northern Ontario that the only guy who appeared to work there helped me with my luggage and then waved his arms to signal the plane for takeoff with Sophie's diaper bag slung over one arm. Then he drove me to the reservation where I was expected.

Funding ran out and I received my first pink slip. But the success of this popular history initiative helped me, at the tender age of thirty-two, to get a job for which I was barely qualified, as the executive director of a brand-new labour museum. I had applied for a programming job, but the hiring committee wanted to give me a chance in this role, although they talked me down ten grand in salary to make up for my inexperience. I was a quick learner, and a year later got that ten grand back when my contract was renewed. The learning curve was vertiginous, and I absolutely loved it. I worked in a beautiful heritage building, facilitating the creation of art that reflected the lives of real people. It brought together all the things that mattered to me. Initial funding for the museum had been generously provided in the dying days of Ontario's New Democratic government, which was replaced with a lean, mean, catastrophic period of populist right-wing rule. Everything and everyone but the very rich suffered. I lost my job, and from that loss, never fully recovered. My mobility shifted downward.

I went to forty interviews in the summer of 2000, and it began to dawn on me that my career path was going to be full of potholes. I had missed the window to get a nice secure job as a translator or a policy analyst in the civil service, not that I was cut out for that life. But I wasn't cut out for digging in my coat pockets for subway fare either.

I finally found another wonderful job with an agency that used popular theatre to engage homeless and marginalized youth and helped them get some skills and stability in their lives. My colleagues were both passionate and compassionate. But it was still the era of deep spending cuts and political contempt for social services, and we couldn't survive. A couple of years after that agency closed came Toronto's first infamous "summer of the gun," where gang violence made daily headlines. Pundits pondered, "How are we failing these kids?" I shouted at the TV, "By cutting the programs that gave them hope, you assholes!"

This loss crushed my spirit, and I took a break for a couple of years. Of all the unlikely jobs, I became manager of a fitness studio. I'd taken up Pilates to deal with the physical reality of being forty, and when I lost my income, I had the nerve to ask the owner if I might barter for my classes. She asked what I knew how to do. I said, "Run organizations." So, she hired me, and even paid for me to train as a Pilates instructor myself. I liked teaching, even if my students were rich ladies looking to strengthen their core muscles so they could play better golf, but pretty soon the job felt too uncomplicated. Apparently, I am attracted to perplexity and repel money. I was wooed back to the third sector by a national feminist organization. Its purpose was to fundraise on behalf of various feminist groups with mandates ranging from women's skills training to legal support for women inmates. It seemed like a very sound idea, perhaps with a future.

But my unerring ability to pick a job that would be defunded with the next change in government continued: federal support was pulled as soon as Stephen Harper became prime minister and set about undermining women's equality. After this layoff, I was just plain pissed off. I was done rolling boulders uphill year after year and seeing my hard work obliterated. I decided that if my work was going to be precarious, I'd at least set my own terms. Rather than being vulnerable to the vagaries of political change, I'd throw myself upon the mercy of the marketplace.

I have loved making things with my hands since I was a little kid. My after-school job as a teen was at Lewiscraft, a chain carrying arts and crafts supplies, where employees were expected to be proficient with virtually all the materials in the shop. This explains why, to this day, I can macramé or découpage if called upon to do so. For my business adventure, I imagined a space where people could be creative even if they had limited time and money. My idea was to offer mostly one-off workshops for grown-ups in everything from knitting and embroidery to screen printing and bookbinding. I knew this wouldn't generate enough income, so I added a retail side, selling handmade goods by Ontario artisans. I called it Wise Daughters Craft Market. I loved being beholden only to myself and interacting with quirky creators every day.

You'd think people would dig this, and they did, but not enough to choose my shop over Walmart or online bargains. I was a little ahead of the curve. I like to imagine that I helped inspire the handmade mania that now fuels Etsy and has even spawned a craft reality show with two of my favourite entertainers, Amy Poehler and Nick Offerman. Many visitors treated my shop as a gallery and a source of inspiration without opening their wallets. Everything I offered was reasonably but appropriately priced, ensuring that the artists were fairly compensated.

Over five years, I sold enough to make a difference to the artists, but there was nothing left to pay myself. I spent the whole time moonlighting, either taking contracts with not-for-profits or writing relentlessly cheery shlock for a local community paper.

I sunk a whole lot of money into the start-up, borrowing against my house. My equity wasn't bad, after I'd sold my house to buy half a lesbian love nest with my partner, so I had access to a lot of credit, which was a dangerous thing. The business grew slowly but steadily, but then the whole retail sector took a hit, and I was too close to the bone to hang on. I no longer had anything to borrow against, having been turfed from the aforementioned lesbian love nest without warning. I was devastated to have to close. I had met wonderfully talented people and gotten to know a small but dedicated group of regulars who became close friends, expanding my social circle more than at any other time in my life. I know these are the riches that count, but it stung just the same.

I thought I'd be able to go back to director-level work in the not-for-profit sector, but the combination of my age and my lack of a graduate degree landed my otherwise fully loaded résumé on countless reject piles. I was shocked that I couldn't get an interview once I'd passed the half-century mark. Many people warned me this would be the case, but I scoffed. Doesn't everybody know that postmenopausal women should rule the world? Apparently not. Amy Schumer has written a very clever sketch about a woman celebrating her last day of being "fuckable" in Hollywood. In it, Julia Louis-Dreyfus goes off in a rowboat, crossing over to the other side of fuckable, cheered on by female peers enjoying flutes of champagne. I found it funny until I realized that *fuckable* and *employable* are two sides of the same coin, and not just in the entertainment industry.

By the end of 2014, having sent out two hundred job applications, I had a new experience: I went on welfare. I explained about my over-fifty/no-Master's situation, and the employment counsellor brightly suggested I go back to school not five minutes after ascertaining that I was broke enough to get social assistance. I wasn't embarrassed, but I was demoralized and had a lot of trouble resisting regret. After many years of inadequate income, I had also racked up considerable debt on necessities like groceries and prescription drugs—and had to declare insolvency, which is one step down from bankruptcy. There was a certain poetic justice in wiping out a swath of the money I owed the big banks roughly equivalent to the interest they'd squeezed from me over the years. But it sucks to be a grown-up with a shit credit rating. Radical acceptance is a process that's never finished.

Of necessity, I began doing the only job for which I am highly sought-after—nannying. Turns out people are keen to snag a progressive grandma-type to mind their kids. The lesbian thing might actually be a bonus—a feather in the cap of urban liberal parents. I remind myself that childcare is an essential service, and the little ones remind me about joy. I wish I could be looking after kids whose parents really need me, rather than those who can afford me (and countless other advantages for their kids), but that's not how things work.

I have only experienced exploitation once; in every other situation, I was treated like family and remained close to my employers once my charges outgrew me. In one disappointing instance, though, the youngish parents who had been so keen to hire me seemed to think that having a nanny brought with it a huge advantage over daycare—the right to abuse flexible hours. My day was contracted to end at 5:30, which quickly stretched to 6:00. We adjusted my hours and pay to wrap a half hour later, which soon meant anytime between 6:00 and 6:30. I didn't mind until Sophie went into hospital; at that point I asked if my employers could observe quitting time, so I could get downtown to see my daughter for a bit before visiting hours ended at 8:00. I wasn't asking to leave early, only on time, but they said no. So, I grudgingly gave my month's notice, as stipulated in my contract.

They decided my services were not required as of that very day and tried not to pay me for my termination period. They were affronted that I knew the law and was not afraid to apply it. We reached a settlement to avoid small claims court. I knew I'd get another gig in short order, given the dire shortage of childcare in Toronto, which I did, at twenty-five per cent higher wages to boot. The terrible part was being torn so abruptly from the wee kid I loved, who must have felt abandoned. We had spent nine hours a day together for nearly a year. The experience made me wonder how many nannies who come to Canada on a domestic worker visa put up with terrible working conditions out of fear of deportation. All the Filipina nannies I have hung out with treat the kids like their own and work bloody hard at a very demanding job. They deserve a shitload of respect.

I have channelled my experience in the not-for-profit world into volunteer work in the LGBT community, sitting on boards of directors instead of reporting to them. To me, fighting homophobia is an obvious extension of fighting misogyny—patriarchy is built on the fear and mistrust of all things feminine, and that includes gay men. Some men don't like lesbians either, because we threaten their sense of purely biological worth and demonstrate a perfectly viable way to live outside the traditional economic structure of the heterosexual nuclear family. But when men display feminine traits or choose male lovers, it threatens the whole premise of masculinity as the dominant force in nature. Because a dominant force needs something to dominate. It's a poor premise, and since it doesn't hold up rationally, it has to be violently protected by those who benefit from it. Trans and nonbinary people simply make the patriarchy's head explode.

I have relished finding community among the people I work with in this new capacity. I have especially loved meeting LGBT youth, so full of piss and vinegar like I was at that age. They think they invented sex, which is adorable, and they use the voice they've been given thanks to the struggles of those who came before to say very interesting things. They challenge my thinking about gender all the time, which can only help stave off dementia.

My volunteer work has kept me connected to the arts, which makes my situation infinitely more bearable. Art is the point. Stuff is not the point. For most of my adult life, I owned a house and a car and lived a middle-class life, not on par with my parents', but not wholly different either. But now I find myself…unencumbered by assets. It's humbling to have lost property that could be worth enough to retire on by now. I have to share what living space I have, like countless generations of women before me. But being impecunious is bad enough without beating myself up about it. I'm not broke because of my own stupidity, but because of choices that made sense at the time (with the possible exception of getting knocked up at twenty-two). I have such a low boredom threshold I would have been miserable in many of the jobs I might have qualified for. I can't stand greed, officiousness, bureaucracy, or inefficiency, which rules out nearly all employment options. Maybe my work wasn't all boulders up a hill; I made my daughters proud, which counts for a lot.

I've moved often as a result of my downward mobility, so I've arrived at the point where I can honestly say I have no superfluous stuff and I know the exact location of each and every one of my possessions. Apart from some photos and ephemera (I am the family historian), my only chattels are items I use regularly. And art, of course. When I buy something other than groceries, I choose carefully, and it's an occasion. Quite often, I can work my way around buying something new—by repurposing something old or bartering. It's been wonderfully liberating to break free of the cult of consumerism. I may need support in my dotage, but at least my family won't have to sort through a cache of ancient rowing machines, juicers, and flatware. What I have is beautifully organized, and I appreciate its minimalism. Most people dread moving, but I think I've been less stressed repeatedly packing up and decluttering than I would be in a home I'd occupied for decades with the detritus of life piling up around me. Those objects would weigh on me, nagging to be culled.

My carbon footprint is small, intentionally and not. I have everything I need and some of what I want. The rest I have let go, along with a discernible waist and any concern for the odd chest hair. Sometimes I go to the grocery store in questionable attire, and I do not give a fuck. I don't wear a bra if it's over twenty degrees, or else I get heat rash under my boobs. If Bette Davis could go bra-less out of fear of breast cancer, I'm not risking hives to protect passersby from the faint outline of my well-loved nipples. The advantage to being invisible as a crone in this culture is that nobody is looking anyway. I swear I could go into No Frills topless and nobody would notice. When I'm well and truly into my golden years, maybe I'll try it.

Number Twelve

MARCH 3RD, 2020, around 8 p.m., Sophie texted me: "Love you lots." I texted back, "That's a nice text to get! I love you lots too." Then she signed off with a blowing-kiss emoji. I had been reading in bed. I briefly thought: is she saying good-bye? But it wasn't at all unusual for Sophie to send me a reminder of her love like that now that our interactions were so positive. I withdrew the question and read a while longer.

Sophie was in a rough place, but we, as mother and daughter, were in a smooth place. Our relationship was better than it had been in a very long time. Sophie had gotten angry with me and chosen to cut me off entirely, from the previous March through September, and it had been a harrowing six months filled with rehashings of all the losses of my life. Sophie could be volatile and hold on tight to a grudge. It was easy to say the wrong thing to her.

But then in September, when she suddenly resumed communication, our ability to express our huge love for one another without clashing had been remarkable. I'd finally gotten the hang of pure validation, unadulterated by snippets of advice, and her communication with me had been free of criticism and defensiveness. Perhaps I had finally absorbed the message my therapist had imparted years before: "As impossible as it feels to be Sophie's mother, imagine how impossible it feels to be Sophie." We were finding the possible in our deeply enmeshed, trauma-filled lives.

Sophie sent a few other texts that evening—ordinary, chatty messages—to her sister and to her fiancé. Also to her drug dealer, to thank him for the fentanyl that had taken away her pain. She was—fleetingly—feeling good, maybe even well. I will never fully get this. I once took a single Percocet I'd been prescribed after surgery and hated the high so much I couldn't wait for it to subside. But my daughter had to live in a very different body than I do; she was always at risk for addiction. I couldn't even get addicted to cigarettes as a teen. In this regard, I am simply lucky.

Earlier that Tuesday, Sophie and I had communicated by text and online several times, which was normal. She was going to see her doctor that afternoon to review for the umpteenth time whether there was anything different she could try to combat both her mental and physical pain without one remedy creating a whole new set of problems, as so often seemed to happen. We had talked at length on the phone on Sunday, when she had confessed to a relapse with heroin a couple of weeks earlier. I reacted calmly, as I always did, and she reacted gratefully to my calm, as she always did. I had sent her a public health warning about a spate of fentanyl overdoses that weekend in the town where she lived. She replied, "Thanks, Mum. I do know about it. I'm not using, but it's still good to share." I don't know if she'd already picked up the fentanyl from her dealer at that point.

֍

On March 4th, at 8 a.m., when the cop phones me from outside my apartment door (I was already at work), I have pushed the worry of the previous evening so far down that my first thought is that there has been a break-in. But he tells me Sophie has died during the night. I crumple and wail. I haven't wailed like this for thirty years. I don't know how I'll ever stop or stand up and support my own weight. But eventually I do. My beloved fairy godson comes to collect me and stays with me until Emma and her family arrive from the west coast the next evening. I have to speak to the coroner, who tells me there was evidence of drugs at the scene. I tell him about the blowing kiss emoji. I say suicide is a strong possibility. But I'm not sure—it doesn't sit right—because I know Sophie would never purposely let her fiancé find her body. She had overdosed once before, and he had rushed her to the hospital. I believed, her sister believed, and he believed that she would never want to put him through that again.

I have to make a series of excruciating phone calls over the next couple of hours. Whenever I say the words, "My daughter has died," I leave my body and hear myself talking from some distance away. It is disconcerting but I assume this phenomenon will pass, and after that first day, it does. I fall asleep in the afternoon. I will sleep a lot in the coming days, my body and brain involuntarily but mercifully shutting down at regular intervals. I am so grateful for this stress response.

I can't stop wondering what my daughter felt when the second dose of fentanyl hit her system. I can't stop myself from Googling in search of what I want to be true. Let it have been instant, my mind repeats. Evidence suggests it was—her chair overturned, her food and drink spilled. She had some art supplies on the table. She had taken lamb chops out of the freezer to thaw. She must have intended to cook them the next day. She must have intended to be here to cook them the next day.

Small holes spontaneously appear in my skin. They look like spots where something jabbed me. After a while, they close over. I also get patches of hives and rashes. An area of my surface will suddenly itch like mad, as if to remind me I'm still here. Months later, I still get mysterious bumps and lumps and sores that appear and disappear. The huge hole that will never scab over is not visible.

My hair starts to turn white. Its pigment hung on for a good long time, but this vestige of my youth now bids me adieu; every time I see myself in the bathroom mirror, there are more and more colourless strands among the blond. One day I notice that my eyelashes have become completely invisible, and my eyebrows are quickly disappearing too. I look old.

I talk a number of times to the lead investigator, who has unlocked Sophie's phone and tells me that her texts back and forth with her dealer outline a clear plan to manage her pain on an ongoing basis with fentanyl. The cop is convinced that Sophie didn't mean to die. She tells me that what so often happens is this: one hit of fentanyl feels amazing. It also impairs the ability to measure time and quantity, so the next hit is fatal. Concentration in the illicit version is wildly unpredictable, and much of it is also laced with deadly additives. That's how Sophie became overdose number twelve over a very short period in the small town of Guelph, Ontario. Two of the overdoses were fatal; many of the victims were saved with Naloxone. But Sophie was home alone, her fiancé working his weekly late shift. I think the emoji was just in case.

For nine days after Sophie's death, I had my other grown child to cling to. We could spoon on my spare bed and indulge in a communal sob for as long as it took. I could hug my baby granddaughter, and the friends who brought food, and my daughter's devastated fiancé. We were able to gather—about a dozen of us—to talk about the young woman we had all loved and lost. On that day, March 14th, gatherings of more than 250 people were discouraged. By the next day, there were rumblings that getting together in groups of any size was perhaps ill-advised. The day after that, everything started to stop.

My surviving child and her family flew home to the other side of the country. We had no idea we wouldn't be in the same city again for months. And I was suddenly solitary, confined to my apartment. While I wasn't paying attention, the whole world went on bereavement leave with me, and now we are all "in this together." Only what I'm in is different. Everyone is trying to keep their loved ones alive, but I'm too late for that. I am painstakingly keeping myself alive because my family is already way too small.

Left alone, I no longer dare to sob uncontrollably. I take control of all the objects surrounding me, culling them, organizing them, moving them, storing them, placing them just so. I take control of my food intake—enough but not too much. I take control of my torso and limbs by moving them around a bit so they'll keep functioning. I take control of my brain, offering it distraction and enough stimulation that it won't start seeping out of my ears. My senses barely engaged, I remain "ok" because I don't know what the alternative to "ok" looks like, and I don't want to know.

❧

From the time Sophie had picked up her life after her long hospital stays in 2018, she had fought for her health like a gladiator. She had returned to university part-time but had not been well enough to write her December exams; somehow she reviewed the material and aced them the following June in order not to lose the credits.

She started and either quit or got fired from several jobs. She was in no shape to work, but her disability benefits from the government barely covered groceries, so she had to bring in some money. And she had a powerful work ethic; she wanted to be able to hold down a job. So she just fucking did it—she answered ads and went to interviews and tried as hard as anybody has ever tried to do anything. Sophie had been working, as a volunteer or for wages, since she was thirteen. She was good at jobs. She was perhaps better at telling people what to do than being told what to do (the apple doesn't fall far from the tree), and received some painful employee reviews as a result. But she suited some employers perfectly for the same reason, because she could be left unsupervised to get stuff done and get it done well.

In January, after a major panic attack at a job she'd just started, she conceded that she had to take another break and went back to volunteering once a week with a peer support program, attending as best she could. For a brief moment, she let the relief of not having to work wash over her. She taught herself to crochet. She tried weaving. The last time I ever saw her, she popped by for craft supplies after a doctor's appointment in Toronto, and we talked mostly about fun with yarn. She found temporary enjoyment and comfort in these activities. She reached out to friends explicitly to prevent isolation. She cooked gourmet meals for her partner.

But I was afraid she was losing sight of her future. She was so frustrated that she hadn't finished her degree yet.

She knew that it would take little effort on her part to earn her few remaining credits. Academics were her jam, even hampered by lingering memory loss from all the electro-convulsive therapy she'd received (a "shit-ton," as she put it). But she didn't know when she'd feel well enough to study again. In a gesture that defines bittersweet, the University of Guelph awarded her degree posthumously.

She had become engaged a year before, and longed to get married, but was concerned about the cost of a wedding, and seemed to be losing the energy and enthusiasm to plan it with each passing month, as her depression deepened. One of her worst fears was that she shouldn't or wouldn't be able to have children, because she was too ill. The thought broke her heart because both she and her partner wanted so much to be parents. Sophie threw herself into adoring her baby niece and showering her with gifts. But I knew the tenderness she felt was both love and loss.

This is the obituary I wrote, sitting at my dining table at 4:30 in the morning a few days after her death:

On March 4, 2020, 27-year-old Sophie Margaret Breen was the 12th person in a matter of days to overdose on fentanyl in Guelph, Ontario. Her cause of death makes her one of far too many. But to her family and friends, she was one of a kind: a powerfully intelligent, passionate, talented, independent, resilient woman.

For many years, through terrible suffering caused by mental and physical illness, she did absolutely everything in her power to heal and to be healthy. She found the strength to resist drug misuse for the better part of six years. When she was feeling well, her impact, her achievements, and her lust for life were formidable. When her depression worsened, she mustered all her strength to try to dig herself out of it, and she never stopped seeking help. Nor did she ever stop offering help and advocating for those around her. She experienced severe and chronic physical pain, and after trying everything else, one night she was desperate enough to take a terrible risk in the hope of finding even a moment's relief. For that, no one can fault her.

We, her family and friends, can take comfort in the fact that Sophie knew she was deeply loved. She was generous with her appreciation of this love—especially the love she received from me, from her sister and from her fiancé, whom she looked forward to marrying with great joy. She loved us back, fiercely. Sophie did everything fiercely. And we are going to honour her memory fiercely.

We chose to place Sophie's death notice on social media as well as in the newspaper; we all agreed to make it clear how she died, for the simple reason that smashing stigma about mental illness and drug use had been one of her prime objectives in life. She would have been ashamed of us if we reported that she "died suddenly" and left it at that. What happened next took us by surprise. My post was shared by individuals and groups across Canada, appearing on dozens of health sites. Hundreds of people who had known Sophie wrote to me. A bunch of people I didn't know and who hadn't known Sophie wrote to me, some having seen only the newspaper obituary. Media outlets asked for interviews, and I gave them, even though it knocked the stuffing out of me, because I wanted to do right by her. I wrote a radio essay for *The Sunday Edition* on CBC; its overwhelming response told me that silence and stigma are still endemic, and deadly.

One journalist asked me how I felt about the arrest of her dealer, which he had reported, and how I wanted to see justice done. I had to think carefully about what I wanted to say. I knew the guy; he was an old boyfriend of hers, from long ago. Sophie had told me he was in active addiction and she had been trying to help him. I was sure he was devastated by her death; his arresting officer told me as much. I was glad that his product was off the street, which might prevent a few deaths for a few days. I was taken aback to learn he might be charged with manslaughter or criminal negligence causing death. I hoped he would get treatment if he ended up in jail.

But ultimately, how could justice possibly be served? Did the dealer do something wrong? For sure. But he is like the tiny patch of sidewalk in a 2000-piece puzzle of a cityscape. Did the people who manufacture illegal fentanyl and sell it on the dark web do something wrong? These fuckers I'd like to stop in their tracks, but even their role must be understood in the context of big pharma's aggressive and immoral creation of the market for opioids in the first place. Did the doctors who couldn't find a fix for Sophie's complex illness do something wrong? I think they used all the tools at their disposal, and it's not the tools' fault they are woefully inadequate.

It's easy to let blaming and shaming immobilize us. We need large-scale, wholesale, massive change in the way we understand the human brain and treat human pain. For that, we need science and we need compassion. We need to fight capitalism and to prioritize human need over human greed. It's no small undertaking. But nobody should ever be told there is a three-year wait for an inpatient program unless you've got tens of thousands of dollars to pay upfront. Nobody should ever be told there are no beds but you're welcome to sleep on the waiting room floor. And nobody should ever have to resort to an illegal, unsafe drug supply to ease their suffering.

Family Emergency Rate

WHEN I FOUND MYSELF abruptly single, my posse of women friends gathered around me and did a multitude of things to help, both major and minor. I had never had a large number of friends, going for quality over quantity; I had been quite timid in my younger days, and also too busy to socialize much. But the arts business I ran for five years attracted a magnificent collection of creative women. Some came to sell their handmade wares, some to learn a new craft, and some to appreciate the skill and beauty of others' work. They became good friends; I ended up rich in human assets, if not the other kind.

After my ejection from Club Crone, they helped me move and gave my bachelorette pad a thorough house-warming that involved the consumption of every ounce of alcohol in the place, right down to the cooking sherry. They were just there, sometimes to fulfill roles a partner would usually play, like picking me up after I had my wisdom teeth out late in life or taking me to the hospital while I was passing a kidney stone, barely able to speak from the pain, and barfing profusely in the friend's car. I never felt alone in those first months post-breakup, and I still don't.

When I took in a foster teen, my friends welcomed her with cards and gifts, hung out with us, taught her cool stuff they knew how to do, and slipped me yoga passes when it became apparent I needed to decompress. They were our village.

The first time Sophie was in crisis and in and out of hospital, I was back and forth to Guelph constantly, and on a moment's notice. My friends covered for me at my shop, one generously charging me the "family emergency rate of zero dollars per hour." They lent me cars, slipped me bottles of wine, and simply had my back. I was aware, even in the midst of the chaos, what an invaluable gift I had in these friendships.

When Sophie first needed a residential treatment program, available only on a fee-for-service basis, the price tag was just shy of twenty thousand dollars. In mama bear mode, I unabashedly sent pleas for help to anyone of means within my circle of family, friends, and acquaintances. To my utter shock, the affluent spouse of someone I volunteered with wrote me a cheque for the full amount. Just like that. We barely knew each other; we had met at events a handful of times. It was a stunningly beautiful gift. Just the fact that a stranger would be so generous lifted Sophie's spirits.

Once, I showed up on the doorstep of the friend who had staffed my shop for zero dollars, sobbing because the car rental place around the corner wouldn't let me take a vehicle without a credit card. (I was in a period of insolvency but taking drastic measures to put my financial house in order.) Without batting an eye, she dropped whatever she'd been doing, hopped in her car, and dropped me at the hospital where my daughter had been urgently admitted, in a whole other town a full hour and a half away.

And when Sophie died, the floodgates opened and support gushed in. I will never be able to properly acknowledge the kindnesses—from small and meaningful to huge and overwhelming. I received Air Miles points and tiny acorns decorated with Japanese paper, mountains of food and lines of verse. Although I sometimes feel like the perpetually needy one, I know that I reciprocate the generosity of my friends as best I can with what I have. I use my organizational skills and knack for finding free art events to bring my friends together. I throw great potlucks. I offer simple pleasures. And anyway, nobody is keeping score.

Twenty Twenty

THE YEAR 2020 will go down in history as a year of agonizing pain and a year of long-overdue reckoning. How fitting that this is the year the dominant culture in North America had its blinders torn off and was forced to address its impaired vision. I hope revolution is coming and I'm sad Sophie won't be here to see it. I wish I could hear her calls to action and see her fighting against oppression in her own inimitable style. I can picture us protesting side by side, as we have so often, my pink diaper baby and me.

In March, Sophie died, and everything came to a standstill; those two events were unrelated, but not to me. There was so much death all at once, from Covid-19 and from drug poisoning, as the harm-reduction programs, safe consumption sites, and health centres all but shut down. In many Canadian provinces, overdose deaths spiked until they were outstripping coronavirus deaths by staggering margins. Toronto's drug deaths increased 85 per cent over the previous spring.

At the same time, in the US and Canada, it felt like there was a never-ending series of murders of Black and Indigenous people by police. Many of the victims were people in emotional distress. I couldn't escape the memories of my own family members' encounters with police when they were having mental health or drug crises—three family members, from three generations—during which no one was ever injured, much less shot dead. There but for the grace of white privilege. Grief and anger overwhelmed the continent.

This was the context for my decision to take the smallish risk of getting on a plane to Vancouver in July, which I weighed carefully against the projected benefit of being with Emma, her partner, and my granddaughter, Andie. I had to visit with them outdoors at a distance at first, but ultimately got to touch a human for the first time in four months. We had held a small, private gathering for Sophie immediately before the lockdown orders came mid-March, and then everyone had quickly scattered to grieve in isolation.

Prior to crossing the country, I had not really considered that Vancouver was the last place Sophie, Emma, and I had all been together. We had met there in December for the holidays. Walking the same sidewalks Sophie and I had strolled, I was battered by an onslaught of memories. I thought about every detail of our final meal as a trio, a sushi feast in Gastown. The calendar was fraught with triggers as well: I arrived just before the fourth of July, which marked four months since Sophie's death and the seventeenth anniversary of Dan's. Emma's thirty-fourth birthday a couple of weeks later represented the milestone of half her life without him.

I accepted that I had to let in a second wave of grief and knew that writing would help me ride it out. I had allowed myself unlimited grief days in the early weeks, knowing sleep would bring respite and I would get a breather before the next one. I never had to fight the grief, because I had the luxury of time and unemployment to wallow in it. If I found myself resisting some necessary emotion, I knew I'd have a chance to deal with it during my weekly grief appointment with peer support counsellors from the Distress Centres of Greater Toronto. While out west, I was able to continue with my trauma survivors support group run through the same agency, since life had moved online due to the pandemic.

One memory I had held mostly at bay for two years was that of Sophie's first drug overdose, this one intentional. It happened in June 2018, after she'd spent weeks and weeks in hospital, and came on the heels of our rather frantic Mother's Day quest for help. One night, about ten days after her most recent discharge, she took a great many pharmaceuticals, but not in a combination or quantity to cause permanent physical harm. When I got to the hospital, she was unconscious but stable, talking quite a bit in her sleep. At one point she mumbled quite audibly, "Take the shrimp off the printer before they burn!" I kept needlepointing by her side. She suddenly opened her eyes, looked right at me, and said sternly, "I'm talking to you!" I assured her I'd see to the shrimp, but she was already off dreaming about something else.

After twenty-four hours, she was moved from ICU and Emma arrived from Vancouver. It was the second time that spring that she'd suddenly rearranged her life to fly to her sister's bedside. Sophie was pleased to see her but didn't seem to fully understand why she'd come until her head was clearer the next day. She was discharged as soon as her vital signs were normal, though she was by no means well enough or safe enough to be on her own. Emma, Sophie's boyfriend, and I worked to remove everything dangerous from her apartment. We had to confiscate her wallet so she couldn't buy anything sharp. Her prescriptions had to be renewed every seventy-two hours so she couldn't stockpile. For several days, we basically took turns guarding her. It was unbearable and untenable. We took her back to the hospital.

She was kept for just under a week, and during this time her condition suddenly improved. Nothing especially different happened in terms of treatment. It was as if she'd touched bottom and somehow pushed off and came up to the surface again. She was referred to a new daily outpatient program that she attended through the summer. Emma went home. She and her partner decided to try for a baby; I danced around my kitchen when I got the news in September. Sophie's partner stayed the course, offering unconditional support and love as he always had.

Later that fall, Sophie asked him to marry her and he said yes. For a brief while, talk turned to baby names and engagement rings.

In my trauma support group, I felt different from the other mourners in two significant ways. One was that I was not plagued by guilt. Thanks to a good mother, decades of therapy, and a great deal of specialized learning, I knew that I could not have prevented what happened on March 4th. One could not say that Sophie's death came as a shock to me. I hadn't expected it, but as I found myself telling one reporter, when someone has a serious chronic illness, fear of relapse is never far away. Medically speaking, her prognosis had never been great. She was dealing with too much. That she managed for so long, achieved as much as she did, loved people and received love in return, was a testament to her iron will.

I also felt alone in my support group, and sometimes just in general, because I don't believe in an afterlife. I may be entirely without spirituality and I'm okay with that. But I do feel a twinge of envy when I hear others talk with conviction about the continued existence of their loved ones' souls, or about their tangible feelings of connection to the departed. Some refer to their loved ones as angels and believe they are at peace; some see signs that they interpret as communication from beyond. I experience no such comfort. I have never sensed the presence of my mother or daughter. I think about them constantly; they are always in my mind's sidebar or scrolling just below my conscious thoughts. I dream about them vividly, and often. Just once that I can recall, I had a very cinematic dream in which my mother, daughters, grandchildren, and I were all reunited. We didn't end up in paradise, exactly, but in a very pleasant and serviceable dormitory in the countryside. At least I woke up feeling like we were all okay. I was interested to note that my mother had taken up turquoise jewellery-making while passing the time.

I've joined Moms Stop the Harm, a national group for mothers who have lost children—many in their twenties—to drugs. It is the last group anyone would want to join, with one of the fastest growing memberships in Canada. From these fierce women I have learned to describe Sophie's cause of death accurately, because language matters. She died of fentanyl poisoning. This is what I want the uninformed to understand, like the troll who commented on the CBC website that my daughter was a "junkie," after hearing my radio essay about grief. There may be no cure for severe assholery, but there is a cure for ignorance.

In this year of forced accountability, I choose to remain hopeful that the vast inequities threatening humanity will continue to be challenged by social movements more widespread and sustained than we've seen in a long time. Sophie herself continues to demand change with the power of a gut punch that I could never have foreseen; her beautiful face has been displayed on a big, bright, digital billboard in Ottawa during the weeks I've been writing these last paragraphs about her life. August is overdose awareness month around the world, and Moms

Stop the Harm has made people turn to look at the youthful faces of our dead on billboards across Canada. Each of them lost in a fraction of a second.

Acknowledgements

The first, very raw draft of what would become this book was written in five days at the end of 2014, during which I never took off my pyjamas. It coincided with one of my rare depression relapses. Then it sat, minding its own business, for a good year. Slowly, it began to take the form of distinct stories, which eventually reunited again to form a whole.

Both of my daughters read various drafts and were willing to revisit and discuss some very painful experiences, and to let me share stories that are not just mine to tell. Without their love and generosity, this book would never have left my computer in the first place. Its writing felt like an act of resistance from the beginning, but most ferociously after Sophie's death, when my anger needed words, and the words needed to combat the stupidity and stigma that are killing our young adults. I rewrote the ending to Sophie's story frantically at first, during the peak of my grief. As the weeks and months passed, the writing became a way to mourn. Thank you to David Schatzky for explaining to me that grieving is what happens internally, and mourning is what we put out into the world. It is grief gone public.

I have been supported all the way along by my circle of women. An early draft was read by the author Nancy Jo Cullen, who had enjoyed a good literary year and wanted to pay it forward. Another draft was given a reading by theatre artists Shannon Bramer and Cathy Gordon, when I was wondering briefly if it should morph into a play. Still another draft was critiqued by the author Alison Pick, who organized free consultations for emerging writers in response to the #MeToo movement. She expressly wanted to help a single mum, and chose me, for which I am eternally grateful.

I read a version of the chapter about my Etobicoke childhood at the Naked Heart queer literary festival in Toronto in 2017, where editor Gillian Rodgerson, an alumnus of SEE School, recognized my description of our counter-culture alma mater and urged me to finish the rest of the manuscript. I thank Gillian with all my heart for championing this book from start to finish. It has been a joy to work with her at Second Story Press.

This book is based on my own memory and interpretation of events. I have been truthful to the best of my recollections, but these are subjective and may vary from the recollections of others, naturally. I thank my cousins

Anne Boadway, Enid Hunt, Mary El Milosh and Karen Townend for sharing research, anecdotes, and ephemera that filled in missing pieces of my family history. Many thanks to the "Randorks" for letting me write at their lovely lake house.

I want to thank Josh Wales, Lisa Schultz, Cathy Thorne, Whitney Sweet, Jonathan Seinen, Meg Masters, Roberta Samec, and the Junction Writes group for their generous critiques, suggestions, and words of encouragement. As soon as I told one friend I was working on a book, she sent me fifty bucks, unsolicited, as a show of faith. I have not forgotten this kind gesture and have done my best to put her investment to good use.

About the Author

MARY FAIRHURST BREEN grew up in the suburbs of Toronto and raised her kids in an artsy, slightly gritty part of the city. A translator by training, she spent thirty years in the not-for-profit sector, managing small organizations with big social-change mandates. She also launched her own arts business, indulging her passion for hand-making, which was a colossally enjoyable and unprofitable venture. Its demise gave her the time and impetus to write her family history for her daughters. She began to publish autobiographical stories, and wound up with her first book, *Any Kind of Luck at All*.